UP
STAND
ING

UPSTANDING

UP STANDING

UPSTANDING

FRANK A. CALDERONI

ANAPLAN CEO

HOW COMPANY CHARACTER CATALYZES LOYALTY, AGILITY, AND HYPERGROWTH

WILEY

Published by John Wiley & Sons, Inc., Hoboken, New Jersey.
Published simultaneously in Canada.

For general information on our other products and services or for technical
support, please contact our Customer Care Department within the United States at
(800) 762-2974, outside the United States at (317) 572-3993 or fax (317) 572-4002.

Wiley publishes in a variety of print and electronic formats and by print-on-demand.
Some material included with standard print versions of this book may not be
included in e-books or in print-on-demand. If this book refers to media such as a
CD or DVD that is not included in the version you purchased, you may download
this material at http://booksupport.wiley.com. For more information about Wiley
products, visit www.wiley.com.

Library of Congress Cataloging-in-Publication Data is Available:

ISBN 9781119746492 (Hardcover)
ISBN 9781119746553 (ePDF)
ISBN 9781119746560 (ePub)

Front Cover Design: Georgina Brown

SKY10025970_042121

This book is dedicated to…

My father, who taught me the meaning of upstanding character

And to Jessica and Matthew, whom I hope maintain his legacy

Contents

Foreword

I first met Frank in early 2012 over breakfast to explore his interest in joining Adobe's Board of Directors. It was clear from that initial conversation that Frank was a pioneer of understanding the critical connection between corporate strategy and culture in driving a company's success, as his criteria for making a decision were not only limited to Adobe's strategy, but also considered our values, culture, and character. Over the past eight years, as both Audit Chair and Lead Director of Adobe's Board, Frank has provided tremendous insight to the company as we navigated our own business transformation. Frank's expertise and counsel have been invaluable to me personally, as I have evolved in my role as CEO.

Throughout his illustrious Silicon Valley career, Frank has led transformational initiatives for iconic technology companies, including IBM, Cisco, and Anaplan, during critical junctures of growth. Frank has a growth mindset and runs his business by the numbers, but he also understands that people are a company's greatest asset and that employees do their best work when they resonate with the mission and values of the company.

In *Upstanding*, Frank examines the inextricable link among corporate strategy, company culture, and individual character, underscoring the significant role every employee plays in embodying culture and contributing to a company's long-term growth and success. Activating that link is essential to realizing strong company character—and a requirement for organizations aspiring to achieve hypergrowth, agility, and loyalty. Frank's assertions are reinforced with compelling stories from his own career—as well as other highly successful leaders in his network—and he outlines a practical set of principles that can serve as a blueprint for companies seeking to develop, nurture, and sustain strong character. He posits, and I wholeheartedly agree, that strong character is a proven way to increase employee satisfaction and productivity, and ultimately, win in the market. I've seen for myself the positive impact that character has on organizations, including Adobe.

Being CEO at Adobe has reinforced for me the importance of a company's character. This was clearly the case when, nearly a decade ago, we set in motion how to transform our business from a profitable packaged software company to one of the software industry's largest and fastest-growing subscription businesses. We knew we had to pivot our strategy and business model to achieve strong long-term growth, but we also knew it would not be easy. Without our employees' belief and commitment in our transformational vision, it would not have been possible. Adobe's sincere and encouraging culture played a critical role in bringing people along, and supporting our character built the bridges of trust needed to carry us through the transition—igniting our passion and determination to succeed.

Frank is right in stating that now more than ever, a company's success is not only defined by its financial performance, but by the role it plays in making the world a better place. A company's social purpose, ethics, and commitment to sustainability, diversity, and inclusion are as important as the products it makes. Companies must consider and support all constituents—employees, customers, partners, investors, and the communities in which they operate.

Dynasties are built when great people are rallied around a great mission, culture, and values. The confluence of these factors enables innovation to thrive, businesses to succeed, and the world to move forward.

I hope you'll enjoy *Upstanding* as much as I did.

Shantanu Narayen
Adobe Chairman and CEO

Introduction

"Sometimes the longest journey we make is the sixteen inches from our heads to our hearts."

—*Elena Avila*

Upstanding company character is essential to achieving and sustaining peak performance.

I've learned more in the last 18 months than in 35 years in business. The combinations of a global pandemic, recession, and social justice movements are unlike anything we've experienced in our lifetime, and we're all dealing with the heightened expectations that employees, customers, and investors have of the business sector to lead the way through *daily* change. But these conditions have accelerated a huge shift that demands action if you and your business want to remain relevant.

How you show up, what you stand for, and what actions you take to that end—as an individual and as a leader in your organization—are now gating factors to lasting success. Today, the degree to which what you say and what you do are tightly aligned will often be a stronger success indicator than traditional professional or business fundamentals. There was a time when we separated our personal and professional personas, leaving opinions unrelated to work at home. Those days are gone.

People are holding companies accountable for societal, environmental, and governance practices with little to no patience for inaction. Growing and protecting brand value, whether it's for consumers or business-to-business, is contingent on organizations navigating uncharted waters of social change in hyperpolarized communities. And every one of us is making choices about what to buy from whom, driven not only by product or service quality, but by whose values align with our own and speak to a shared purpose.

The year 2020 was a moment of truth for character. And I'm proud of how the employees at Anaplan—the company I lead—persevered. Our ongoing emotional investment in living our values enabled shared *resilience*. Resilience that fueled our leaders and teams through the worst of circumstances. What we drew on was an *upstanding character* that we knowingly—and sometimes unknowingly—created to guide us with clarity and cohesion.

While the multiple crises of 2020 underscored the renewed and urgent relevance of company character, the cumulative factors, previously outlined, which affect all businesses and have led to this moment. To help navigate our shared experience, I wrote this book drawing on the artifacts and experiences I've cultivated as a leader. I've assembled wisdom from experts and peers in my network, included notable stories from business headlines, and shared methods to develop your own versions of *upstanding character* for your organizations. As a result, this book offers ways to think about company character, culture, and actions you and your teams can take to lead effectively now.

I definitely don't have all the answers, and I don't get it right all the time. But I am willing to keep trying. It's imperative we all do.

How I Got Here

I'll never forget my first real job. I was 20 years old during the summer between my sophomore and junior years at Fordham University, where I was working on a degree in accounting and finance. I applied to IBM for a position as a summer intern, went through a pretty rigorous round of interviews, and was accepted. Little did I know at the time what an impact this temporary summer job would have on my future. And never could I even imagine it shaping my views as a future CEO.

Getting hired by IBM, even for just a few months, was a really big deal for me and my family. At the time, IBM was still the 800-pound gorilla of the computer industry, and the company was well known as one of the most successful corporations in American business. In 1979, the company was ranked No. 7 on the Fortune 500 with annual revenues of more than $21 billion and profits of more than $3 billion. By way of comparison, then No. 1 General Motors had three times more annual revenue—$63.2 billion—but "just" $3.5 billion in profit.[1]

I repeated my internship with IBM the following summer, and when I graduated, I accepted a full-time position with the company. I ended up working at IBM for 21 years, building a career that helped me get established at Cisco Systems and set the stage for my future growth as a leader. And while I have worked for—and led—some amazing companies in the years since, IBM and Cisco both made a tremendous impression on me, and I have carried a piece of each with me.

Let me start with IBM. The overarching mantra at IBM when I was there was a deep and abiding respect for the individual and the community. And not just for those who were employed by IBM, but respect for individuals who were part of our business ecosystem—partners, vendors, and customers—and respect for the people who lived and worked in the communities in which we did business. As new employees, we were taught about the history of this great company, and we were steeped in its values and culture. In fact, there was a company song we knew called "Ever Onward," the official IBM rally song.

IBM's culture was built on a firm foundation of what it called the *Basic Beliefs,* introduced by then-CEO Thomas J. Watson Jr. in 1962:

- Respect for the individual;
- The best customer service in the world; and
- Excellence.[2]

I quickly came to appreciate this remarkably deep, people-focused culture. I learned at IBM how pivotal a clear, pervasive culture is to the success of any business—no matter what industry it's in, where it's located, or how large or small it might be—and how hard it is to sustain performance when times get tough in the absence of strong shared core values.

My experience at IBM also taught me what can happen when leaders fail to honor, promote, and renew a company's culture. IBM faced a very real crisis of confidence in the 1980s as the computer market shifted from the large mainframes that provided most of the company's revenues and profits to small desktops. In 1986, earnings declined 27 percent and revenues dropped precipitously. During the course of six years, 170,000 employees were laid off or retired, budgets were cut, business lines were discontinued, and the pension program was slashed.[3] As IBM's business results became more challenged, new people were brought in to run the operation, and they didn't take advantage of the culture as an asset to drive and accelerate a required reformulation of IBM's business strategy. Instead, the business changed the culture, and this negatively affected the business.

Of course, IBM wasn't alone during this time—many other stalwarts of American business conducted layoffs, cut benefits, and restructured their operations. According to *The Economist*, in the decade after 1987, approximately 3.5 million American workers lost their jobs due to downsizing.[4] The focus of many companies moved from people to the bottom line, and the focus remained there for the better part of two decades as the dominant mindset of corporations.

Make no mistake about it—growing sales and profits was always an important part of the IBM mindset, but historically, this growth was considered to be a natural result of following the three Basic Beliefs. If you respect employees, provide the best customer service, and demand excellence, IBM would grow—and grow and grow.

At IBM, I started out in finance, and I was fortunate to be invited to join a special management development program for individuals with strong leadership potential. A key part of the course was a talent assessment to determine early in our careers if we had the attributes that would be required to lead IBM into the future. As you can imagine, the pressure to excel in the assessment was intense. We were tasked with working through complex business cases—problem solving, developing strategies, working as part of a team, presenting, and writing. Through it all, seven or eight assessors closely watched everything we did that week; how we managed ourselves determined our career progression. As an introvert, it was a hugely stressful pressure-cooker experience that pushed me to be more extroverted. While it felt way outside my usual comfort zone, it also thoroughly engaged my competitive instinct—I could win at this!—and it was formative to shaping my leadership drive.

The course and assessment were rigorous, but they were also helpful and revealing. When we received our results, we learned exactly what we did well, what areas we should work on to improve, and we had a much better idea of our potential as future leaders at IBM. Excellence was expected and the bar was set high. I eventually worked my way up to Vice President, Finance and Operations for Global Small Business, making me the senior financial and operations executive for a $3 billion international brand and customer organization. And it was at IBM that I learned firsthand the value of how to work with cultural differences.

I was born in America, but I'm a child of immigrants. My father immigrated to the United States from Italy when he was just five years old and settled in a small, rural town in New York State with *his* mother, father, and brother. Like many immigrants at the time, they went through Ellis Island.

My father went to college, but he left before he received his degree—he needed to work to provide for our growing family. He had a strong work ethic and worked long hours as a tradesman to give us a good life. My mother didn't go to college—she stayed home to take care of me and my two brothers, Bob and Rick, and later developed a career as a computer technician after we left home. We lived comfortable lives—we weren't affluent by any means, but we didn't lack for anything.

I think my father always regretted not getting his degree, so he impressed on my brothers and me from an early age that we would definitely be going to college. I started working when I was 12, delivering newspapers, and my brothers started working at a young age too. The expectation our father set for us was that the money we made would be put into savings for college. The main focus, however, was on studying and doing well in school.

When I was in high school, everyone was talking about going to college, but I didn't fully understand what college was all about. My parents didn't have experience with the college and career landscape to help fill in the gaps, so my brothers and I had to learn as we went through the process ourselves. We had to figure out what schools were available to us, how to apply, and what professions to pursue. I decided to talk with my high school guidance counselor about it.

The guidance counselor asked me a few questions and then he handed me a list of colleges. "Go look at these," he said. "You may want to think about going to them." I didn't realize it at the time, but that counselor set the path to my future.

Fordham was one of the schools on the list. I liked that the school was in New York City, and it had a strong reputation, especially for business careers. Going to school in New York City was an eye-opening experience for me. I was somewhat sheltered growing up in a small, rural town with my family, but at Fordham, I started getting more engaged in the community around me.

I wanted to try different kinds of jobs, so I worked for a hospital (a short-lived tour as an operating room technician) and a radio station while I was in college. The station broadcast throughout the Tri-state area—New York, New Jersey, and Connecticut—with a variety of music and news programming to reach multiple niche audiences. I was initially interested in majoring in journalism or the arts at Fordham, so I decided to become a business reporter at the radio station to explore both professions. I was exposed to the corporate world, and this was my first experience on how companies reported earnings.

While I was at the radio station as a news reporter, I had the opportunity to interview some significant people at the time, including President Jimmy Carter, Vice President Walter Mondale, New York City Mayor Ed Koch, and other political and business leaders. I would be standing in the press scrum trying to get in and hold up my microphone along with all the big networks: ABC, CBS, and so on—which were big moments for me as a small-town kid. I was learning firsthand about politics and business, and it opened up a whole new world to me. Those experiences were as valuable as the formal education I was getting in college. As much as I loved the creativity of working at the radio station and doing some film-making on the side, my rational side said I needed to go into business so I could get a good job out of college. So, I decided to major in accounting and finance.

As I neared graduation, I started knocking on doors in New York City, dropping off copies of my resume at companies I was interested in. The very first job offer I got was a full-time finance position from CBS at $12,500 a year, and I still have that first offer letter to this day. Although I was excited to receive the offer, I decided to wait and see if IBM would make me an offer following my summer internships. Luckily, the company made me a full-time job offer.

My education continued as I moved up the ranks at IBM. I started in an entry-level job, but I had the good fortune to socialize with different levels of people in the company and met several executives whom I personally aspired to be like, and who became mentors. I was really interested in leadership early in my career. There was something about helping people develop their skills and advance in their own careers that spoke to me. Within just a few years, I was promoted to manager and led a team of eight people.

When I joined the finance leadership team for IBM's EMEA (Europe, Middle East, and Africa) division, I spent most of my time in Europe. After that, I was tasked with overseeing finance for the San Jose–based storage business and I moved to California. The division invested heavily in Asia operations so I spent a lot of time traveling in China, Singapore, Thailand, and other Asian countries as we expanded disk drive manufacturing throughout Asia.

I learned professionally and personally by traveling extensively at a time when U.S. businesses were just entering previously inaccessible markets. I have vivid memories of walking on the Great Wall of China, boarding a Russian Navy ship in St. Petersburg, and bartering in Indian markets.

I had many interactions with customers and other IBMers around the world, and they were often very open to showing me around and sharing different parts of their cultures—what was most important to them. Through these experiences I learned that cultural understanding is essential for doing business.

Although most of my fellow business students at Fordham had a goal of working for one of the large, public accounting firms upon graduation, I ended up accepting a position at IBM because the company really cared about its people. They focused on ensuring we connected as coworkers. They had a number of clubs, sports teams, family outings, and as someone starting a career, this was a wonderful way to learn more about colleagues by sharing hobbies and building relationships. We felt like a family; we felt like we belonged, and that has resonated with me ever since. I built many long-standing friendships that have stayed with me through today. I even met my wife, Brenda, at IBM, where we were colleagues growing our careers in the finance organization.

However, I recognize that during that era, for all IBM's strength of character, the company had accepted norms that by today's standards were biased against diverse people. While women and Black team members were not uncommon, my colleagues were predominately white men, especially in the more senior positions. And an uncomfortable truth during that time was that people of color and women were systemically disadvantaged. Thankfully, the IBM culture has evolved, as has the mindset of most leading businesses around the world, but we still have so far to go on inclusion, which I discuss further in Chapter 7.

This year alone has confirmed without a doubt that when you make character the foundation of everything you do, and when you're more inclusive of diverse people and backgrounds, you're a much more effective business leader. You benefit from different perspectives that result in far more equitable and innovative products. You develop trust, relationships, and partnerships on a whole new level, which in turn, drives loyalty and growth in your business.

I joined Cisco in 2004 as Vice President, Worldwide Sales Finance, when the company was in its heyday, and was promoted to CFO in 2008. Profits were soaring, business was great, and some of the best people I have ever worked with were joining in record numbers. During my tenure, the company more than doubled business revenues and profits. But then we faced major adversity in the wake of the global recession, which hit in 2008–2009 and affected Cisco for several years. I will never forget the day in 2011 when we received 11 analyst downgrades, lost billions in the marketplace, and suddenly had a lot more adversaries.

This was a time of significant company transition. Cisco had more than 66,000 employees globally and a very strong company culture. We had to quickly implement a cost-savings plan in excess of $1 billion—leading to heartbreaking rounds of downsizing and layoffs—while at the same time trying to maintain a positive culture. It was probably where I learned the most about how important culture can truly be when the worst happens all at once.

Throughout it all, our Chairman and CEO, John Chambers, set a remarkable example for others in the company to follow. During an earlier downturn, he had reduced his own salary to $1 a year.[5] And while other employees volunteered to take pay cuts to reduce layoffs of their coworkers and help save the company, John declined—deciding that morale would suffer.

As CFO, I both felt and observed up close the pain that the downturn was causing my colleagues on the executive team, and how difficult it was for us to make hard decisions that affected people's lives but were necessary for survival. But I could also see our collective character that was the foundation of the Cisco culture. It would have been easy for all the pressure—both internal and external—to bring us down, but we stayed above it. And while it's normal to react to challenging circumstances, you shouldn't let that change who you are as a person.

I learned a lot about character from the entire Cisco executive team. It was a learning experience for all of us as we made and implemented the hard decisions required to get the company back on a firm financial footing. One thing that helped was that the standout trait of the Cisco culture was optimism. In fact, a *Businessweek* article about John Chambers published six months before I joined the company described him as "irrepressibly optimistic."[6] Regardless of what was happening in the world around us, we knew we were going to persevere; we were going to win in the long run. Leaders didn't have to threaten or badger people to work harder. Everyone seemed extremely self-motivated. We understood that we needed to lift ourselves up and continue forward, so that we could get ourselves back on top.

We had a common purpose that came from our strong core character. My time at Cisco demonstrated how the strength of company character provides an unwavering foundation to carry a business through the hardest of times.

As we all know, growing sales and profits are essential for sustained financial performance. But leaders who focus narrowly on financial results without a parallel focus on culture and organizational health may be surprised when they hit the inevitable iceberg. As job markets have tightened in recent years and great employees are harder to recruit and retain, companies have had to put the focus back on people. Competition for talent is one factor forcing a return to the importance of character to business. Many more realities at play require leadership teams to build culture for sustained advantage and resilience: intertwined global markets, the power of social media to make or break corporate reputations, digital transformation, and the imperative for cross-functional connectivity and collaboration.

As business leaders, we implicitly know the importance of strategy—of setting goals and then developing plans that help us achieve those goals. This is very much a "hard" science—we can measure and quantify the results of our strategies and determine whether they have been successful. For many, the focus on creating a positive organizational culture is a "soft" science—something much less quantifiable, perhaps impossible to measure. The result is that leaders typically default to emphasizing strategy over culture, hoping it will lead to the results they seek.

Of course, it's not that easy, especially if you are going through the kind of turmoil we experienced at Cisco back then. While there's no denying that strategy and "making the numbers" are essential, research overwhelmingly shows that an organization's culture significantly affects employees' engagement—their passion and commitment to making the company successful. I have learned firsthand that employee engagement flows directly to the bottom line. As numerous studies have shown, organizations with high employee engagement perform better in almost every metric compared to organizations with low levels of employee engagement. More on those studies is offered in Chapter 1.

So, if it's not all about strategy, and it's not all about culture, then what really drives performance? **Making culture instrumental to your strategy.**

Competitive agility, hypergrowth, and customer loyalty require combining culture and strategy so they're two sides of the same coin.

After more than 10 years with Cisco, I left for Red Hat, where I became EVP, Operations and CFO. While I was at Red Hat, I learned valuable lessons too. The culture at Red Hat was considerably different from the more structured IBM and Cisco cultures in which I had built my career. Like the open-source software that is its hallmark, the Red Hat culture was also very open to an extreme—in a good way.

In an open culture, I learned about the power that comes from cultivating an openness to feedback that is not curated or reviewed in advance. To allow employees to ask any question, and to allow yourself the vulnerability to answer in a way that is authentic and unscripted. It generated passion and heated debates like nothing I have ever seen before in an organization. It was refreshingly different and something I knew I was going to adopt as I moved forward. These key learnings from Red Hat were what I brought along with me when I became President and CEO of Anaplan in 2017.

Anaplan, the company I lead today, makes cloud-native SaaS software for global enterprises to orchestrate successful business performance. But more than that, it's an organization that I've had the privilege of shaping using all of the insights about character, culture, and leadership I've gained throughout my career.

On my first day at Anaplan, I thought to myself what an honor it was to become the CEO at this up-and-coming startup. Our headquarters was in an industrial part of San Francisco—in a building with retrofitted brick walls, little enclaves everywhere, and a hip vibe throughout. What I learned in the interview process to become CEO was that Anaplan had an incredible product, a large greenfield opportunity, and loads of potential. It was everything you wanted in a startup.

However, it seemed like Anaplan's culture and character were not well developed. Employees enthusiastically supported customers and were clearly passionate about the product, but values were individually defined and culture was fragmented with competing centers of control. There was a need to strengthen values cohesion, inclusion, and shared purpose for the company. I saw this as an opportunity to leverage my experiences with the lessons I have learned along the way—lessons I now feel compelled to share with you, especially today.

Company character is the core that grounds culture and strategy—it is the persistent through-line of fundamental beliefs and values uniting people and teams working with a shared purpose. While our world and business environment are in a constant state of flux and change, the qualities that constitute good character never change. They're timeless.

Character comprises the qualities and behaviors that define us as people—such things as empathy, courage, authenticity, integrity, honesty, and respect. They are embodied in how we work every day, how we treat others, and how we treat ourselves. Organizations that internalize and live and demonstrate *upstanding company character* in every interaction are the organizations that will win today—and into the future.

It is essential—and now more than ever—for business leaders to consider the implications of culture and company character for their respective business. This book explores the crucial intersection of culture and strategy, and how today **upstanding company character** is essential to achieving and *sustaining* peak performance.

PART I

It's a New World

CHAPTER 1

A New Given: Culture Is Strategy

"I came to see, in my time at IBM, that culture isn't just one aspect of the game, it is the game. In the end, an organization is nothing more than the collective capacity of its people to create value."
—Louis V. Gerstner, Jr., former Chairman and CEO, IBM

Leaders must put character at the center of everything they do.

Today, peak performance requires a dual focus on culture and strategy, especially in this new era of doing business. We are in a unique environment marked by instant gratification, pervasive social media influence, and fast-changing global political and economic forces that require every business to be agile and ready to shift at a moment's notice. In addition, the forces of digital transformation and disruption are exerting tremendous pressure on entire industries—and the executives who lead them.

On top of all that, we've all witnessed the tremendously negative impact the COVID-19 pandemic has had on people, businesses, and the global economy—surpassing the downturn of 2008. While many companies have recovered from the severe and unexpected disruptions to their business operations, many others have gone bankrupt or have closed their doors permanently. Major companies filing for bankruptcy during the COVID-19 pandemic include Neiman Marcus, JCPenney, Virgin Atlantic, Hertz, 24 Hour Fitness, Pier 1 Imports, Brooks Brothers, Stein Mart, Sur La Table, and even the Cirque du Soleil circus arts live entertainment company. The list goes on.

And, as I write these words, mortgage delinquencies are the highest they have been in a decade,[1] American Airlines announced that it is going to cut 19,000 jobs,[2] and it was reported that 54 percent of San Francisco storefronts—the local lunch spots, neighborhood grocery stores, fitness studios, and other small businesses that we at Anaplan headquarters regularly frequented before the pandemic—are no longer in business.[3] Internationally, according to Roberto Azevêdo, Director-General of the World Trade Organization, "The unavoidable declines in trade and output will have painful consequences for households and businesses, on top of the human suffering caused by the disease itself."[4]

Clearly, the aftereffects of COVID-19 will leave lasting ripples on how businesses are run and how leaders prepare their companies for the future, perhaps for decades to come. These ripples won't be felt just in the United States, but all around the globe. Every CEO I know is considering flexible new ways of working that put less focus on having people on-site in traditional offices, and more focus on outcomes. And so are employees. According to one survey of more than 750,000 employees working in more than 100 global enterprises—representing every major industry—in early April 2020, 33 percent of those surveyed said they wanted to return to the physical workplace full time post-COVID-19. At the end of June 2020, only 4 percent of those surveyed said they wanted to return to the physical workplace full time post-COVID-19.[5]

It seems that change is all around us.

Leaders intuitively know a great culture enables great business results, and a significant amount of research confirms this. However, that same research shows that most organizations are falling short when it comes to culture.

According to Gallup, which has been regularly surveying the state of employee engagement for almost two decades:

> Culture is a critical part of an organization's identity. Culture is created through the experiences that employees have with the corporation and, just as importantly, with each other—the everyday interactions with peers, managers and executives.[6]

When employees identify with and are aligned with a company's culture, they feel they belong to an organization that is inspiring, purposeful, and truly values their contributions to the team. They feel *connected*. And this connection flows right to the bottom line. A 10-year review of more than 111,000 employee surveys conducted by Aon Hewitt and Queen's Centre for Business Venturing (QCBV) revealed that organizations whose employees have the highest levels of engagement achieve:

- 65 percent greater share-price increase;
- 26 percent less employee turnover;
- 100 percent more unsolicited employment applications;
- 20 percent less absenteeism;
- 15 percent greater employee productivity; and
- Up to 30 percent greater customer satisfaction levels.[7]

This is all good news for businesses with great cultures, but there's a hitch. According to a 2018 PwC survey of more than 2,000 people in 50 countries, although company leaders tend to think their companies have great cultures, their employees don't necessarily agree. While 63 percent of C-suite and board members surveyed reported that their organizations have strong cultures, only 41 percent of employees responded that this is the case. In addition, 80 percent of respondents said that in order to succeed, grow, and retain the best people, their organization's culture needs to evolve within the next five years. Compare this to just 51 percent of respondents in 2013 who said that their organization's culture needs to evolve.[8]

As the Aon Hewitt/QCBV study demonstrates, a corporate culture that is lacking correlates to lower levels of employee engagement, productivity, and business results, along with higher levels of turnover and absenteeism. However, it gets even worse. Gallup also found that 51 percent of employees surveyed are actively looking for a new job or watching for openings at any given time—in many cases because they are convinced that "the grass is greener" in a different organization.[9] Unfortunately, this group of people may very well include your best employees—some of whom may leave before they realize their full potential in your organization.

In 2019, job and recruiting site Glassdoor published the results of its latest Mission and Culture Survey. This survey asked a simple question: What makes employees around the world satisfied at work? According to the results of the survey, the top three drivers of employee satisfaction are:

- Culture and values;
- Quality of senior leadership; and
- Career opportunities.[10]

The Glassdoor survey also revealed that:

- Well over half (56 percent) of employees and job seekers say company culture is more important than salary when it comes to job satisfaction.
- Almost 73 percent of adults surveyed would not apply to a company unless its values align with their own personal values.
- Nearly 4 in 5 people would consider a company's mission (79 percent) and culture (77 percent) before applying for a job there.
- Almost 2 in 3 employees (65 percent) say company culture is one of the main reasons for staying at a job.
- 65 percent of U.S. Millennials are likely to place culture above salary, which is higher than any other age demographic surveyed.[11]

Clearly, culture matters and has a tremendous impact on who joins and stays at your organization—and ultimately, on your ability to execute strategies required to achieve the goals you set for your organization.

When I became CEO of Anaplan in 2017, I could see the culture needed an overhaul. Even though our product was exceptional, and we were on to something that had enormous potential, that was not enough to make the company successful long-term. One thing I noticed early on was the company was lacking in diversity and inclusion—in fact, internally the nickname

---

Company Culture Is Distinct from Company Character

Company culture is the system of beliefs, values, goals, behaviors, and the way employees feel working in the organization—from leadership style, decision-making norms, customer experience, and company policies—officially and unofficially. Essentially, it's the personality of the organization. Culture evolves over time, often adjusts with leadership change, and must be actively managed.

Company character is the integrity, respect, and fortitude residing at the core of your culture. It is the basis of trust and emotional connection people have with your organization—measured by the distance between what you say and what you do. Company character is the timeless alignment of your values (your stated intentions), your reputation (what you're known for), and your actions. It is earned as much as it is defined.

"Manaplan" was often invoked because upper management of the company was mostly men, and women were not well represented across functions.

We needed to make some changes quickly to transform Anaplan's operations and culture. I will get into the details of that transformation later in this book. But for those of you who are trying to understand your culture, I recommend asking these questions: How does your culture evolve amid ever-changing business, political, social, economic, and customer dynamics? How does your culture remain clear, consistent, and powerful amid hypergrowth? How does your culture persist when people are dispersed globally, expect more from work, and work remotely?

The New Relevance of Character

What we know as someone's character anchors the relationships we build with people around us—our boss, the people who work for and with us, our customers, our vendors, our investors, the communities in which we do business, and the world at large. Positive business reputations rely on leaders and cultures with upstanding character—behavior that demonstrates values people can rely on and build trust in. From what I have learned, character is intrinsic and enduring—like a boulder that weathers a hurricane with no visible stress or damage—and the origins of the word reflect this.

Character found its way into our language from the ancient Greek word *charassein*, which means "to engrave," as you would engrave a letter, number, or other character onto a surface such as clay, wood, or metal using a chisel. As the pioneering psychoanalyst Dr. Richard Sterba pointed out, this original meaning has since been broadened to humans. Says Sterba:

> Character designates the features of personality which are more or less indelibly engraved upon it, features which of course express themselves in actions and reactions, features that are "characteristic" of the individual, features by which one ego structure can be differentiated from others.[12]

I believe that, just as a great culture creates competitive advantage, so too does defining and nurturing an *upstanding* company character. Companies with upstanding character embrace and embody the virtues of empathy, courage, authenticity, honesty, integrity, respect, and more. All of those attributes combine to create positive interactions and relationships that are then rewarded with loyalty, engagement, and goodwill. People make decisions on what to buy, where to work, whom to partner with, and whom to affiliate with based on a company's values and on the character (or lack of it) displayed by its people. Do you stand for something? Is your focus on making the world a better place or just on making money?

We all have our personal opinions on which companies stand out when it comes to character and living their values; there are a variety of annual surveys that rate the best places to work based on employee feedback. For example, rankings for the annual *Fortune 100 Best Companies to Work For* are based on the results of a 60-question survey given to workers at companies with at least 1,000 U.S. employees. According to the Great Place to Work organization, which administers the survey, 85 percent of the evaluation is based on what employees report about their experiences of trust and reaching their full potential as part of their organization, no matter who they are or what they do. The remaining 15 percent includes an assessment of all employees' daily experiences of the company's values, people's ability to contribute new ideas, and the effectiveness of their leaders, to ensure they're consistently experienced.[13]

Here are the top three companies on the 2020 list and a sample of what employees had to say about these organizations. It will be interesting and instructive to see if the organizational stresses brought about by the COVID-19 pandemic have a significant impact on the upcoming versions of this annual list.

- **Hilton.** "I love how I don't feel like just a number here. I am a strong believer that Hilton cares about their employees just like they care about their family and I am truly blessed to have been given the opportunity to work for such an amazing company."
- **Ultimate Software.** "Ultimate Software takes care of its people and genuinely believes that putting people first is the only way to succeed. I have never felt more supported in my role or happier to come to work than I have since I started my journey with Ultimate."
- **Wegmans Food Markets.** "When management says they care about their people it actually shows in their actions. I have always been made to feel wanted and valued as a person and employee."[14]

I can almost guarantee that all companies on the *Fortune 100 Best Companies to Work For* list have strong, positive cultures and that their leaders have character and are fully aligned with their organizations' values. There are, of course, companies that have done well financially—sometimes incredibly well—despite having bad reputations and creating negative environments for their employees. But they are the exception, and the good results don't last.

The kinds of behaviors that were once considered "par for the course" in some organizations—underpaying women, celebrating aggressive "bro" cultures, excusing bad bosses, stigmatizing LGBTQ+ employees, marginalizing people of color—are no longer tolerated. People don't want to work for companies like this; they don't want to buy products or services from companies like this, and they don't want to support companies like this.

Consider the example of Uber, the disruptive ride-sharing pioneer that achieved a valuation of $70 billion by 2016, just seven years after it was founded in 2009.[15] This valuation was truly a remarkable financial milestone, but there was a very dark side to this accomplishment. Uber's problematic culture, endemic in the engineering team, was revealed in 2017 when former software engineer Susan Fowler wrote a blog post about her experience of sexual harassment and discrimination at the company and her unsuccessful efforts to get management to do something about it.

By the time Fowler made her viral blog post, more than 200,000 people had deleted their Uber accounts—many to protest Uber's perceived support of the U.S. government's travel ban of January 28, 2017, and also the company's negative culture and then-CEO Travis Kalanick's alleged role in creating and perpetuating it.[16] According to one Uber executive, employee morale cratered after these incidents. "Until 2017, you could go into Uber on any given day and half the T-shirts were Uber T-shirts. They disappeared overnight. People didn't want to wear Uber stuff."[17]

In June 2017, Kalanick took an indefinite leave of absence, and he was ultimately pressured to step down as CEO by five key investors (he remained on the Uber board of directors until 2020). Uber's next CEO—Dara Khosrowshahi—joined a few months later and immediately got to work on reshaping the company's tarnished corporate culture, creating a more stable work environment, and stemming the exodus of talented employees. Even so, three years after the CEO transition and after publicly acknowledging that its culture was detrimental and in need of change, Uber continues an uphill battle to repair its reputation. This is a textbook example of how an unmanaged culture can cause real reputational and financial damage to an otherwise promising company.

Leading for Character and Culture

I have had the benefit of experiencing different corporate cultures at the companies I worked for and those of customers and partners that I interacted with. There is one consistent feature that distinguishes cultures that personally resonated for me. A strong positive culture guided by upstanding core character has always been highly motivating for me as an individual— an environment in which I wanted to connect, but also to perform. I felt like I *belonged*. I was part of something bigger than myself, doing good in the world, and I wanted to do well—not just for myself, but for the organization and for our customers.

When good character grounds culture, people are more energized and motivated to do well. The leaders set the pace. There's openness, so people understand what's expected of them. There's collaboration, so everyone works together. Drama, office politics, toxic behavior, and other negatives are discouraged and kept to a minimum. I've personally seen and experienced the impact of a strong culture that's created by people demonstrating a core character that made me feel included and valued, and consistently generated great results.

In my experience, leaders who embody upstanding character trust and respect the people who work for and with them, and this trust is reflected right back to them. Trust is built when we say what we believe and we follow it up with action. Employees say to themselves, "I'm going to do whatever I can for them because I like what they stand for. I believe that they're here on my behalf." And, so, a lot of the behavior that I saw over the years in the people I respected as strong leaders and mentors, I tried to emulate myself as a leader, and I tried to model in the various roles or responsibilities that I've had.

So, who defines a company's character and culture? It's the employees themselves—everyone who works for the organization. And I believe at the heart of an upstanding character are two simple qualities: trust and respect. It allows for psychological safety so that you feel comfortable to speak up, disagree openly, or offer a completely different suggestion knowing there are no repercussions. When trust and respect are strong, people tend to commit fully, and they are less distracted by the unimportant, petty issues that plague so many organizations—destroying the energy and motivation of employees—while putting their focus on the important things that are positive and really make things happen.

After the big downsizings and layoffs of the 1980s and 1990s, when the markets turned around and companies started to hire again, technology companies started bringing back the kind of perks that we thought people wanted—particularly in the Silicon Valley. We started to offer free food, recreational facilities, dry cleaning, on-site childcare, Ping Pong tables—all sorts of pluses to attract and retain talent by creating a pleasant environment. But at some point, we began to realize that we needed to go much deeper than those superficial niceties. We needed to think hard about creating the kind of environment where people would truly connect and feel a sense of belonging—and where they could grow and realize their highest aspirations.

While people work in an organization to make money and further their own careers, they also get to socialize, communicate, collaborate, and learn new and different things. The environment plays a critical role in that, and a company's environment is tangible. You can sense something about a company's character and culture just by walking through the front door. Part of it has to do with how the environment looks and feels. Is it open and inviting? Or are people divided and closed off? You can see it in how people carry themselves and how they occupy their space. Are they engaged and active—excited to be there—or would they rather be somewhere else?

Here's an example of what I mean. One night, before the first COVID-19 shutdown, I stayed late at the office and decided to get something to eat nearby. I was hungry and didn't want to wait to get home for a very late dinner. There weren't many places open, so I stopped by a popular chain restaurant known for its rotisserie chicken. I hadn't eaten at this chain for a long time, but I fondly remembered it for its great food and great service in a friendly, home-like environment.

Unfortunately, the reality of the restaurant had nothing to do with my memories. To begin with, the restaurant was dirty—*really* dirty. It looked like the tables hadn't been cleaned off in some time, and there was trash and food scattered around the floor. The service also suffered—the employees acted like they would rather have been anywhere but there. They were sloppy, unfriendly, and just threw the food on the plate. The entire experience was decidedly unpleasant—for me and for the people who worked there. Whose fault was this?

I can tell you that behind the scenes, this company is not being managed well. They don't have respect for the people who work there, and as a result, the employees don't have respect for their managers or customers. Because, if they felt more respected, they would make sure that they presented themselves better. They would take pride in maintaining a clean and cheerful environment, rather than one that's neglected with food all over the floor. I saw a direct correlation between the company culture and the customer experience. And it wasn't a good one.

When employees are valued by the people who lead them, they feel important, appreciated, and connected. And this applies so much to Anaplan. I hear this all the time when I'm out with customers. I was at an event in London with some of our customers—executives from Jaguar Land Rover. Mike Tickle—Planning Director, Commercial at Jaguar Land Rover—said to me:

> Frank, I don't know if you know this, but the reason why I started looking into Anaplan is because I went to an event and several of your people were there. They were so energized and so enthusiastic about what they were doing that I felt like I would be missing out if I didn't get to know more about what was going on. It piqued my curiosity because of the people and how they were carrying themselves, and the enthusiasm they had for their company. I wanted to be part of it.

Of course, I was delighted to hear this, and it tells me that we are doing some things right. At the same time, I know we're not perfect. Anaplan is a work in progress, and we still have a ways to go. But, working together, we're accomplishing some truly amazing things for our customers, in a culture based on mutual trust and respect. In fact, we've hired a number of people who used to be our customers. In every one of these cases, the people we hired were impressed with the Anaplan culture, which they experienced as they worked with our employees.

Sara Baxter Orr is our Global Head, CFO Practice. Here's what she told me about experiences she had before and after joining Anaplan:

> While I was still with Verizon, you invited me to speak at Anaplan's Women's Interest Network. It was a fantastic event—there was tremendous passion around wanting to help women succeed. And I tell everyone I meet that I've never been around a company where women supported women the way that we do at Anaplan. It's so refreshing and amazing to me because that's not always the case, not every culture is like that. For me, that was very exciting and it's one of the reasons I joined.

And then, after the murder of George Floyd in Minneapolis and the ensuing aftermath, we've really leaned in. We've been honest with ourselves and we've taken a position of wanting to learn, wanting to make a difference, and taking this moment and making it matter. That has been really refreshing and meaningful to me as well. Culturally, this has been just as rewarding as it has been to grow revenue and grow our business.[18]

Ray Curbelo, our Global Head of Finance Solutions, had his own very positive experiences with Anaplan and our culture while he was working at a Fortune 500 insurance company. As he explained to me:

> The Anaplan team I worked with always made it about more than just "what's in it for Anaplan?" It was about what's in it for the customer, how are they going to benefit, and how can they help them be more successful—and help them drive value for the company? It was always simple things, like the account executive at Anaplan sending me articles. He'd say, "Hey, I remember you mentioned you were struggling with X, Y, and Z. This article made me think of you and that situation you mentioned." Or "How is so and so doing on your team? Is there anything we can do to support them?"[19]

Claire Lord, a Senior Customer Success Business Partner, told me about how the Anaplan people she worked with while at Thomas Cook made her and her coworkers feel valued—even after the company went out of business. She said:

> In my role at Thomas Cook, I dealt with a lot of suppliers, and with Anaplan it was never a hard sell—it was always a group effort. You guys weren't selling to us; we were working together. The people that we worked with closely at Anaplan made us feel like we were valued, and they championed us at every opportunity. It wasn't just we were doing our own thing. As a collective, we were working together to make both companies better.
>
> And then, when Thomas Cook went under, we were so overwhelmed by the support that we got from everybody at Anaplan. You know, there was nothing in it for them, but they made us feel like they cared about how we felt. They introduced us to other companies, introduced us to people within the business. And it really felt like they cared about us as individuals, not just as an account. And I see that now from the Anaplan side, which is great.[20]

Our investors have also noticed the emphasis we put on character, culture, and customer focus. Alex Wolf is Managing Director for the Investment Group of Santa Barbara, one of Anaplan's largest investors. In a discussion at one of our large company and partner events, Wolf explained what he and his investment group look for when they assess an investment opportunity, and what they saw in Anaplan.

We spend a lot of time when we get to know a company, trying to understand what they are doing well. We'll ask their customers questions like: Are you happy with the products? Are you happy with the service that you're getting? Have you looked at competitive solutions? Would you ever switch? What would cause you to switch? What other use cases are you interested in buying? All of that checked out extremely well with Anaplan.[21]

Here's an example of a strong culture from a company that everyone recognizes. Disney is famous for hiring young people to work in its theme parks. What's amazing is that the same teenagers who might routinely stay up late playing video games or hanging out with their friends will eagerly wake up at 6:00 a.m. to come to work for Disney with a smile on their faces, ready for the day. Disney claims it's because of the unique culture that it breeds—the pride it builds within employees (called "Cast Members") to do the work that they do, whether it's donning a costume to play a cartoon character, operating a ride, or sweeping litter from the walkways. When they have a purpose and feel valued, they transform from sullen teenagers into stellar employees.

A few years ago, we got a taste of Disney's unique culture when a group of Anaplan leaders participated in a one-week professional leadership and development course at the Disney Institute in Anaheim, California. The leaders were steeped in Disney's approach to building employee engagement and satisfaction while delivering the highest levels of customer service, and they put those lessons to work in their own teams.

A big part of Disney and other companies that leverage culture is that they don't just take it for granted. They put extra effort into it—they make sure that it provides the right business outcomes, just as they make sure their company is delivering the right product and financial results. They'll ask, for example, "Is our employee morale in a good place? If it's not, then we need to focus on that as much as we need to focus on our customers."

In Chapter 6, I devote an entire section to the specific learnings that our people brought back with them to Anaplan, and how we integrated them into our own unique culture.

The Nexus of Culture and Strategy

Culture and strategy are interdependent—they feed and have the potential to elevate each other. When a company's culture ignites passion and loyalty in their employees, their efforts to ensure the success of that strategy are multiplied. The results aren't visible just internally, but externally as well.

In the past, leaders were mostly judged on their ability to execute the technical aspects of their jobs and to deliver results. And while these will always be important qualities for leaders to have, motivating and energizing the people on their team are just as essential. In 2019, *Fortune* published its list of the World's 50 Greatest Leaders. The list represented a big shift in how we view leadership effectiveness today. Instead of being focused solely on financial results, the *Fortune* ranking rewarded leaders in business, government, philanthropy, and the arts who "are transforming the world and inspired others to do the same." And, in the case of the business leaders on the *Fortune* list, they do this by creating great corporate cultures.

On the flip side, some companies do a poor job of creating a positive and sustaining corporate culture, but I would say most are in the middle—they believe they have a good culture but don't actively nurture or invest in it. It is an untapped resource.

What I've seen over and over again are leaders who take their culture for granted. They'll schedule an event that is meant to improve morale, or they'll take on a couple of short-term culture-boosting initiatives, check the box, and then move on. They don't realize that culture is an ongoing, evolving thing that has to be constantly developed and nurtured. Actively demonstrating character and culture starts at the top—it can't be delegated, and it must be intentional.

The second development I've seen is when the singular pursuit of business results comes at the expense of culture, which ends up jeopardizing enduring performance. It's all about how many widgets the company is going to make, and how they're going to make them. They overemphasize efficiency and results—giving culture and people a back seat. Over-indexing on quantitative success will not drive hypergrowth, agility, and loyalty. I know it sounds contrary coming from a former CFO, but you can't sustain your business by managing only to financials.

The third development that often causes culture and strategy to go wrong is office politics and ego. If you don't keep politics and egos in check, bad behaviors emerge, and strategies invariably go awry. Bad behaviors can undermine a culture immediately because they turn people off and shut them down. Instead of being engaged and productive, people take a big step back as they realize they have to play the game. And if an organization rewards politics and ego, these bad behaviors will persist and spread, and have a detrimental effect on culture.

Now more than ever, it's time for leaders in every organization and every industry to put character at the center of everything they do. This character must be based on upstanding values that guide behavior while embracing what has always been good for business—the pursuit of excellence, respect for individuals, and respect for the communities where we do business. The character we exhibit as leaders has a profound influence on the culture of our organizations. And, for hypergrowth, adaptive, customer-centric companies in our era of digital transformation, character-led culture is strategy.

In the chapters that follow, we take a look at exactly how leaders in any organization can define an upstanding character and culture that separate them from the rest of the pack—leading to levels of performance far beyond what you might have ever imagined possible. Now, let's get started.

The Big Nine Values That Drive Great Company Cultures

The MIT Sloan School of Management studied more than one million employee-generated reviews of major companies to determine the cultural values that have the greatest impact on results. Drawing from hundreds of different cultural values, the research effort found that nine stood out as being cited most often. These "Big Nine" cultural values— along with the researchers' definition of each—are:

- **Agility.** Employees can respond quickly and effectively to changes in the marketplace and seize new opportunities. Also known as: flexibility, nimble, fast moving.
- **Collaboration.** Employees work well together within their team and across different parts of the organization. Also known as: teamwork, one company, join forces.
- **Customer.** Employees put customers at the center of everything they do, listening to them and prioritizing their needs. Also known as: customer-focused, deliver to our clients, customer-driven.
- **Diversity.** Company promotes a diverse and inclusive workplace where no one is disadvantaged because of gender, race, ethnicity, sexual orientation, religion, or nationality. Also known as: inclusion, everyone is welcome, celebrate differences.
- **Execution.** Employees are empowered to act, have the resources they need, adhere to process discipline, and are held accountable for results. Also known as: operational excellence, projects managed well, take ownership.

- **Innovation.** Company pioneers novel products, services, technologies, or ways of working. Also known as: cutting edge, leading change, advanced tech.
- **Integrity.** Employees consistently act in an honest and ethical manner. Also known as: do the right thing, be ethical, play by the rules.
- **Performance.** Company rewards results through compensation, informal recognition, and promotions, and deals effectively with underperforming employees. Also known as: meritocratic, recognize achievement, results-driven.
- **Respect.** Employees demonstrate consideration and courtesy for others and treat each other with dignity. Also known as: treat with dignity, courtesy, appreciation for each other.[22]

CHAPTER 2

21st-Century Ethos

"It is said that some people are born great, others achieve it, some have it thrust upon them. In truth, the ways in which your character is built have to do with all three of those. Those around you, those you choose, and those who choose you."

—*Maya Angelou*

Character is the North Star by which we steer our organizations.

We are living in one of the most dynamic moments in history, and I suspect things are going to continue to evolve quickly over the coming years. Change is all around us, and it's imperative that we get ready for change rather than continue to be surprised by it. For years—actually, *millennia*—we have been trying to defy, deny, or slow down change. We need to embrace it. Even the ancient Greek philosopher Heraclitus said 2,500 years ago, "Change is the only constant in life."

It still is, all these thousands of years later.

But what's different is that the kind of change we're going through today is truly remarkable in our lifetimes. COVID-19. Financial uncertainty. Disruptive social change. Natural disasters. And all of it changing daily, not monthly or yearly, but every single day there seems to be something alarming happening. And now more than ever, we are watching to see how companies and individuals navigate these changes and show who they really are. We're asking our leaders, our organizations, our coworkers, and everyone who's important to us what they stand for, and then we're comparing what they *say* to what they actually *do*. And, I suggest, the gap between what they say and what they do is a pretty good measure of their character.

When I talk about character, I don't just mean a list of "core" values that you might see published on a company's website. Character is having the personal fortitude to do what needs to be done to foster the continued growth and success of your organization, your leadership team, and your people. It's challenging everyone—including yourself—to do everything you can to provide your customers with real value, which means doing new, sometimes risky things.

To move ahead, you've got to build on the past but not be stuck in it. As Geoffrey Moore, author of *Crossing the Chasm*, explains, "Technologies from a prior era, once the focal point of innovation, now become the scaffolding upon which next-generation innovation will build."[1] Keep building; keep innovating; keep trying new things. Keep moving forward.

Not too long ago, I spoke with some executives who work for a very large and well-established retail company whose name you would immediately recognize. The organization's culture has deep roots in "doing things the way we always have," and its executives are convinced that continuing to do what made the company successful in the past will assure its success in the future.

Unfortunately, in the case of this large retail company, this perspective (actually, a bias) is holding them back. They are old-school and outdated in their thinking and firmly locked in the past. Their unwillingness or inability to let go of past success is unconsciously stopping them from doing the right thing for the company today—and for their people and their customers. It's hard to watch.

More than a few companies are stuck in a similar predicament. Look below the surface and you'll see that many are on a path to reduced market share and sales, along with declining revenue and profit, public criticism, and perhaps even legal consequences for those involved. Their character is diminished.

Character is the North Star by which we steer our organizations, and it's the scorecard against which we are judged. Our stakeholders are listening attentively to what we say we are, and they're watching what we actually do. In short, they're constantly measuring our character.

When I was on the roadshow for Anaplan's IPO, which took place in October 2018, it was two solid weeks of talking to investors back-to-back. I can remember one investor group in particular that spent a good amount of time in the due diligence with me. While investors asked the usual questions about our business strategy and financial model, they were very focused on the Anaplan culture. They specifically wanted to know more about my personal philosophy and approach. After an extensive discussion, my curiosity was piqued. "Why are you so interested in culture?" I asked.

Their response: "What we have found is that, when you have a strong culture that starts from the leadership and works down through the entire organization, you're going to have a much better return. We've proven that out."

While it's not the entire basis for their investment decisions, a significant part of this investor group's evaluation of whether to invest in a particular company comes from their understanding and appreciation of its values, culture, and leadership. After completing their due diligence on Anaplan—including our culture—they doubled down on their investment. They know that companies with strong cultures are going to execute their strategies more effectively, leading to better results.

We've known for some time that the way companies conduct themselves—demonstrating what they stand for—has become a deciding factor in what we want to buy, where we want to work, and who we want to partner with. A company's character matters to consumers. We've raised the bar for how businesses and leaders should behave for us to continue to support them. The traits and attributes now attracting people to organizations push the requirements of culture beyond simply creating an appealing workplace, stating values, and offering great benefits and perks for employees.

A company's character matters to employees.

Jon Iwata is currently an Executive Fellow at the Yale School of Management, and before that he worked at IBM for more than 35 years—retiring from the company a few years ago as Senior Vice President, Chief Brand Officer. In an interview for *Communication Director* magazine, Iwata pointed out just how important a company's character is to its stakeholders—and to the ultimate success of the enterprise:

> Each company must decide what makes it unique. What does it distinctively do in the world? What value does it alone create? This is the beginning of authenticity—what we call the "corporate character.". . . It is a never-ending process to activate that character throughout the enterprise.[2]

At the intersection fusing culture and strategy, long-term business value is gained, protected, or lost today by a company's character. An upstanding company character is a competitive advantage in a fast-changing marketplace where employees and customers have many choices.

So, the question is this: What's the best way to ensure that character is an integral part of every decision we make?

Let me recommend an answer: by adopting a 21st-century ethos—one that looks to the future for inspiration, constantly keeps a finger on the pulse of relevant trends in the world around us, and considers how they will likely affect our business, our people, and our customers today, tomorrow, and well into the future.

An ethos that puts the focus on *character.*

And, today, every organization needs to live and demonstrate its true character more than ever before—to its employees, its customers, its communities, and to the world at large. The year 2020 was unlike any other before it—a year when we were hit with a trifecta of unexpected events that no one could have predicted. And these events have made business leaders take a deep look inside their organizations to see if what they do is actually aligned with what they say they believe.

First, the global pandemic of COVID-19 brought a wave of illness and death to the world not seen outside of war for a century. The pandemic fundamentally changed the way we do business—with many offices and places of business closed, global supply chains broken, and more employees than ever before working from home. Literally overnight, business leaders were faced with the prospect of managing distributed teams while doing everything they could to keep functioning at some level of normalcy. Companies had to quickly pivot and figure out new ways of working that would allow them to continue to do business.

Second, the COVID-19 pandemic triggered a global recession that threw millions of people into unemployment and undermined investor confidence. According to a Pew Research Center report, 24.7 million Americans lost their jobs from February to April 2020 as the pandemic worsened and the U.S. economy shut down. More women than men lost their jobs during this period, and Hispanic, Asian, and Black women were particularly hard hit.[3] And although the stock market has mostly recovered, the Dow suffered its largest single-day loss ever (2,997.10 points) on March 16, 2020, and the S&P and Nasdaq were also off sharply as investors wondered if we were teetering on the precipice of a global depression.[4]

Third, the murder of George Floyd by Minneapolis police on May 25, 2020, unleashed a tremendous amount of long-suppressed anger—triggering worldwide protests against racism and reinvigorating the Black Lives Matter movement. Business leaders are being held accountable by employees, who are demanding changes not just in recruiting and hiring practices, but also in company policies, marketing, and communication to customers and communities. While many businesses have risen to the challenge—putting their character on full display—others have not, their leaders seemingly out of step with the truly historic events going on around them.

A number of macro-factors are unique to this moment in time, creating a new context that only increases the relevance of company character and adopting a 21st-century ethos. Let's consider some of the most important.

Ethos of Inclusion, Purpose, and Agency

It's not always easy standing out from the crowd and being unlike everyone else around you—at work or in any other part of our daily lives. After a lifetime of feeling different, Ollie Jones-Taylor[5] realized a few years ago what was wrong—a gender identity that didn't match the body he was born with. This realization began Jones-Taylor's gender transition journey (he now identifies as male) to change his body to match his identity.

In so many companies, someone like Jones-Taylor might feel unsupported—afraid to let coworkers know what he was going through. What if colleagues felt uncomfortable working with his "new" identity? What if the work he loved was taken away and given to others? What if his boss marginalized or even fired him? These fears and many more were understandably weighing on Jones-Taylor's mind as he considered whether he could be his true, authentic self with coworkers.

Company values like inclusion, authenticity, and openness are often aspirational—words posted on the wall that may or may not reflect reality. For Jones-Taylor, Anaplan's stated commitment to those values wasn't something he could take for granted; if they weren't real and genuine, his livelihood could be at risk. Could Jones-Taylor trust that his leaders and colleagues would treat him as the same highly qualified, reliable, enjoyable colleague they hired and worked with? Did the company have the *character* to walk its talk?

At Anaplan, those values define how people show up for each other every day. We have tried to foster our Anaplan values to be demonstrated and supported throughout the organization, and lived every day by employees around the world. Jones-Taylor said, "I felt safe coming out as transgender to my colleagues and talking about my transition at work. I feel supported. I'm still just as good at my job. Now I can be my true self."

We all know the importance of character in individuals—being trust-worthy and honest, and doing the right thing. What I've discovered in my career as an executive at IBM, Cisco, Red Hat, and now Anaplan is that character—the qualities and behaviors we are known for—is the corner-stone of corporate culture.

People expect businesses they buy from or work for to be good citi-zens. To value and respect diverse experiences and perspectives. To work for the greater collective good of the communities they operate within and serve. People have almost unlimited choices when it comes to what to buy and where to work, so loyalty must be earned every day of the week.

How people treat each other—colleagues, communities, and custom-ers—matters. I know people choose Anaplan, whether to work with us or buy our products, in large part because of the experience our company character creates for them. We aspire for our people to feel heard, included, and respected, and we hold ourselves accountable to that standard. It's etched deep into our DNA. We work on this every day, and we recognize this work will never end. We have a strong mandate to ensure we keep this an absolute top priority.

The biggest challenge in any organization, but especially large global organizations, is they lose sight of what they're trying to accomplish. Employ-ees end up doing their jobs without really understanding how they fit into the big picture. But when employees can understand what the bigger pur-pose is and how what they do contributes to it, they'll feel more connected. They'll be more fulfilled in what they're doing; they'll raise the bar on per-formance, and customers will benefit.

According to Omar Abbosh, Corporate Vice President, Cross-Industry Solutions at Microsoft, a company's purpose determines its outcomes. Says Abbosh:

> I have absolutely no doubt at all that purpose is super material to the outcomes of a company. Whether it's things like employee engagement or business results, I'm convinced that it's highly material. The way I love to characterize it—and I'm going to steal this from my boss, Satya Nadella—is to look at the difference between a company's espoused values and the lived experience of the people in the company. If that delta is really small, I think the company has a stronger and better character. And, too often, I find that there's a big delta, which in my book is a much weaker and lower character.[6]

So, I'm always trying to understand what it takes to make the delta small between the espoused values—who we say we want to be, presumably because of our purpose—and the actual experience we give people. I think that cultures and leadership styles that are more open, more transparent, that are more soliciting of criticism and accepting of it, are much more likely to be able to close the delta. In my experience, cultures where you have command-and-control leadership cannot have a great character because they don't accept critique and evolution.

Virtual and Global Teams

Virtual and global teams—where people work anywhere, anytime, and often don't routinely see each other in person, if ever—have been just one of the ways we get work done for quite some time now. With the onset of the COVID-19 pandemic, they became the default way to work overnight.

According to a report by OWL Labs, 56 percent of global companies allow remote work, with 68 percent of employees around the world working remotely at least once a month.[7] This widespread adoption of remote work has significantly ramped up over the past decade. Gallup reports that in 2012, only 39 percent of American workers were doing their jobs remotely in some capacity, spending at least some of their time away from their coworkers.[8] By the beginning of April 2020, in the thick of the COVID-19 stay-at-home orders, 62 percent of American workers reported that they were working at home.[9]

While we all know why so many people were forced to work remotely during the pandemic, a clear majority of these employees also expressed their preference to keep working remotely even after the threat of disease passed. Why was this the case? What does this tell us about the way we do business today? How do our actions as leaders affect the way people feel about their jobs and their employers?

What does it tell us about the character of the organizations for which these people work?

I'm certain that, in the wake of the COVID-19 pandemic, how and where we work is going to be fundamentally changed as a result. Not only have a majority of employees said they would prefer to continue working at home, increasingly, many business leaders are coming to the realization that the upsides of remote work outweigh the downsides. In fact, with the digital business tools we now have readily available—WebEx, Slack, Zoom, and many other means of team communication and work—there's less reason today for people to be wedded to a physical office.

Numerous large companies have joined the work-at-home revolution. According to CNN, Twitter, Square, Shopify, Box, Slack, and others have all announced either "indefinite" or "permanent" remote-work status for their employees—often giving employees the choice of whether to continue working this way.[10] In a tweet, Shopify CEO Tobi Lutke announced, "As of today, Shopify is a digital by default company. We will keep our offices closed until 2021 so that we can rework them for this new reality. And after that, most will permanently work remotely. Office centricity is over."[11]

But it's not just tech companies that have led the way. Traditional companies such as Nationwide Insurance, founded in 1926 and based in Columbus, Ohio, have embraced a new work-at-home ethos. The company shut down five regional offices, moving 30 percent of its workforce into a permanent remote-work status, with hopes of eventually increasing this to 50 percent of the workforce. Says CEO Kirt Walker, "Our associates and our technology team have proven to us that we can serve our members and partners with extraordinary care with a large portion of our team working from home."[12]

So, while the trend is toward more remote work, at the same time, we must keep in mind that personal connections are paramount to getting things done. We can't neglect the importance of in-person business interactions in everything from weekly 1:1 meetings to customer visits to informal "water cooler" talk. The lack of face time that is a normal outcome of doing work in virtual and global teams puts all the more pressure on clarity of organizational character to ensure shared understanding of what a team collectively stands for. This poses a challenge to the leaders who are in charge of these teams.

A 2018 survey of more than 1,600 executives working for major organizations in 90 countries found that while 88 percent believed that high-performing global virtual teams are critical to conducting daily work, only 15 percent of the executives who were leaders of such teams rated themselves as very effective.[13]

Building high-performing teams takes a lot of work on the part of leaders, and it takes even more work when the teams are virtual, remote, or global. Leaders must go out of their way to communicate more often, across a wide range of channels—from video conferencing to email to Slack to phone calls to instant messages and much more—to build and maintain strong, long-lasting relationships with coworkers, board members, customers, partners, investors, and other stakeholders.

Making these connections virtually offers us opportunities to build relationships in new ways. For example, turning on your camera when videoconferencing and acknowledging the intimacy of seeing people in their homes, sometimes punctuated by the voices of children, dogs barking, and the swishing of cat tails. There's a real equalizing effect when you're on a Zoom conference with 12 other people and everyone is squeezed into tiny boxes on the computer screen.

Regardless of how and when you communicate, building deep connections with others is *essential*. In 2019, I traveled to Israel to evaluate a really interesting company, Mintigo, that we ended up acquiring. As CEO of Anaplan, pre-COVID, travel was a regular part of my job, and I have met with a wide range of people around the world for a variety of reasons. What was unique about this meeting with Jacob Shama and Tal Segalov, the leaders of Mintigo, was they didn't just tell me about the technology and the team, which were both exemplary, but they revealed details about themselves— who they were as *people*. Without me asking, they told me about their personal lives, their families, where they grew up, what they do, how they came together, and what brings them together as a team—both inside and outside of the office. It was clear the way Shama and Segalov led their team would make for a great culture match with Anaplan. Since the acquisition, the Mintigo team has assimilated well and they now provide a data science cornerstone to Anaplan's differentiated predictive forecasting capability.

The discussions I had with the Israel team gave me a tremendous personal appreciation for who they are as individuals and how they work together as a team. During the course of our meeting, we built relationships that I know will continue to strengthen our partnership for many years. It's easier to do this when you're face to face, but we need to find a way to foster these types of connections virtually as we become even more global and distributed.

The Employer Value Proposition

When I began my career at IBM, it was common for people to work 10, 20, even 30 years for the same company. Today, long-term employee loyalty is no longer the norm, particularly among younger workers. According to the most recent U.S. Bureau of Labor statistics, American workers have a median tenure of just 4.1 years with their current employer. However, older workers—from 55 to 64 years of age—have a median tenure of 9.9 years, while younger workers—from 25 to 34 years of age—have a median tenure one-third that number, just 2.8 years.[14]

If you zero in on individual companies in the tech sector, the stats are even more exaggerated. Amazon has a median employee tenure of exactly 1.0 year and at Google it's 1.1 years.[15]

Why is this the case?

Today, people have more choices about where and how to work, and under what terms they'll accept employment. In competitive fields such as technology—especially for hard-to-fill positions such as security analysts, data research scientists, and database administrators—talent is *scarce*. According to research conducted by iCIMS, from January to May 2019, only 6 tech positions were filled for every 10 that were open.[16] That has implications, both for employers and employees.

The traditional employer/employee contract provided workers with a stable career for a lifetime in exchange for their good work and loyalty. When employees retired, they could count on a pension (a *defined benefit plan*) that would continue to pay them some portion of their salary for the rest of their lives, healthcare benefits, and maybe even a glitzy retirement party and a gold Rolex watch as a parting gift (yes, the gold watch really was a thing).

Under this traditional contract, companies offered stability but not necessarily "meaningful" work. But as long as they upheld their part of the bargain—providing a job (and pension) for life and a steady paycheck—then all was good. When a company went out of its way to provide its employees with a culture and mindset that was more than a transactional relationship, as IBM did during my time there, it was such an anomaly that it was written up as a business school case study.

This classic employer/employee contract began to fall apart in the 1980s. By 1980, the number of American private-sector workers covered by a pension plan reached a peak of 46 percent (35.9 million people),[17] but as of 2019, this number had plunged to just 12 percent of private-sector American workers.[18] Many U.S. employees today have retirement plans that *they* must make their own financial contributions to, such as 401(k)s and the like. Employer-funded pensions are now extremely rare in the private sector.

Which brings us to today, and contemporary thinking about the employer value proposition. To attract and retain the best talent, leaders must think not only about compensation and benefits, but the experience people will have while working at their organizations. Leaders must define the mutual value both the employee and the company will get out of their association together. For professional workers, people change companies and even careers more frequently than ever. Sustaining productivity with that level of mobility means keeping the best people for as long as possible becomes an advantage.

Given the enormous competition for talent that many organizations face today, they must find unique ways to attract and retain great people. This most often takes the form of benefits and perks, rewards and recognition programs, corporate social responsibility efforts, and a distinctive company culture—the things that make an organization a great place to work. When Cisco was named the No. 1 company on *Fortune's 2019 World's Best Work-places* list, it wasn't just because of its pay scales or the fun benefits and perks it offered employees such as free food and drinks in the kitchens and Friday afternoon happy hours. It was, according to the Great Place to Work Institute, because the company had these six elements of a great workplace culture:

- **Community.** Where there is a sense of winning together when times are good and sticking together when times are tough.
- **Fairness.** Where employees feel like everyone is getting a fair opportunity.
- **Trustworthy management.** Where management's actions match its words.
- **Innovation.** Where managers create a safe environment to express ideas, make suggestions, and take risks.
- **Trust.** Where companies show people that they consider them to be trustworthy and give them the opportunity to prove them right.
- **Caring.** Where companies don't just *say* they value employees, they *show* it.[19]

How would *your* organization score against these six elements? Are you making it a priority to create a great place to work—a thriving culture that attracts loyal and high-performing employees—or do you feel it's "good enough" and doesn't need specific attention or investment? As a CEO, I know from my own experience, with research to back me up, that a positive and intentionally crafted workplace culture contributes to long-term success.

Of course, employees must also uphold their part of the bargain. I have worked with Cy Wakeman for many years since my time at Cisco. Wakeman is a business consultant and speaker who pioneered the idea of Reality-Based Leadership—an approach to defusing workplace drama and improving employee satisfaction and performance. Sometimes though, says Wakeman, not every employee upholds his or her part of the employer/employee contract. When measuring employee performance, companies must also pay attention to behavior—to personal character—not just results. "So many people are confused, complaining, blaming, angry, under-responsible for their own affairs and over-responsible for what isn't in their sphere of influence," she says.[20] Wakeman's prescription for this state of affairs is what she calls "Reality-Based Leadership:"

> A Reality-Based Leader (and employee) is one who is able to quickly see and graciously accept the reality of the situation, conserve precious team energy, and use that energy instead to impact reality. Better yet, a great Reality-Based Leader anticipates the upcoming changes and capitalizes on the opportunity inherent in the situation without drama or defense.[21]

People accomplish this by following what Wakeman calls the reality-based rules of the workplace, such as ditch the drama, stop storytelling (negatively speculating based on emotions instead of facts), swim in your own lane, be accountable, and give positive intent.

While the COVID-19 pandemic clearly harmed many organizations, with some going out of business or suffering major setbacks, it has also done some good things for organizations globally. It's opened up the doors to bringing in talent we would never have considered before now that working from home is so prevalent. Commutes are no longer an issue. Also, the strict lines between personal and professional lives have become increasingly blurred. For example, with working parents juggling so much at home, how you manage these people, how you empathize, and how you offer support are key to retaining your top talent.

But the new employer value proposition is a two-way street—employees must also rise to the occasion, and ideally, bring a mindset that it's more than just a paycheck. To sustain a thriving career, workers in all fields and at all levels will need to become adaptable, lifelong learners. Their best experience lies in engaging in the shared purpose of their work, and partnering with their teams and managers to align with the organization's culture, values, and goals.

The Transformation of Every Company in Every Industry

Businesses today are operating in new paradigms that challenge and disrupt long-standing industries. The world's largest hotel booking site doesn't own any hotels. The global leader in providing point-to-point ride service doesn't own any cars. Leading companies and brands can be brought to their knees by a single tweet. And the newest startups can rocket to success based on a viral Instagram post.

Even the most seasoned CEO can fail to see a trend that's going to fundamentally change their business. In 2006, Amazon released its first cloud product: Elastic Compute Cloud (EC2). Larry Ellison of Oracle lived through the rise and fall of "hosting"—which mostly meant clients and servers that sent and received data, services, and applications over a network. When cloud computing came on the scene, my guess is that he figured that he'd seen it all before, and he dismissed it out of hand. In remarks at the 2008 Oracle OpenWorld conference, Ellison said:

> The computer industry is the only industry that is more fashion-driven than women's fashion. Maybe I'm an idiot, but I have no idea what anyone is talking about. What is it? It's complete gibberish. It's insane. When is this idiocy going to stop?[22]

As it turned out, cloud was anything but a fashion statement. It was a remarkably disruptive approach to computing—allowing companies to move their labor- and capital-intensive data centers out of their physical facilities and into the cloud, shifting to a much less expensive pay-as-you-go model that can scale far more quickly and respond to changes in their markets with much greater agility and speed.

And "this idiocy" *didn't* stop. Amazon built Amazon Web Services (AWS)—its cloud-computing division—into a wildly successful business that in 2019 generated more than \$35 billion in revenue[23] while contributing the majority of Amazon's operating income.[24] Notably, Google and Microsoft have also built fast-growing cloud businesses. While AWS's share of the cloud infrastructure market fell slightly—from 34 to 32 percent—from Q2 2017 to Q1 2020, Microsoft's market share rose from 11 to 18 percent, and Google's market share rose from 6 to 8 percent.[25]

While other companies got a head start, Ellison dragged his feet and Oracle was left behind, taking several years to eventually catch up.

Doing things the way we always have, and failing to recognize new threats or industry trends, can lead to costly mistakes. Yes—we all make the best decisions we can in the moment, given the information we have on hand. But this information is heavily biased by our past successes—it colors the way we see the world around us and it has a tremendous influence on the decisions we make. The world of business is quickly transforming in ways we could have scarcely imagined a year—or even a month—ago. It's our job as leaders to keep our fingers on the pulse of this transformation and recognize how we can leverage it for the long-term success of our organizations.

Bigger Data

Many millions of people visit online destinations each and every day—sometimes using their computers, sometimes their smartphones or other digital devices—generating a tremendous amount of user data. This data includes such things as gender, age, race, marital status, political and religious affiliation, net worth, occupation, product preferences, and much more. In fact, data brokers have built an industry based on buying and selling data that is now worth about $200 billion.[26]

In addition to the rapid growth in data over the last 20 years, the nature of this data has evolved over time. First there was no data, next there was too much data, and then there was conflicting data. Throughout all of this, the biggest challenge is that it's almost impossible to find a single source of truth when it comes to trying to focus on the *right* information. And that's exactly where many organizations have struggled. They spent all their effort trying to sort out what the right data is, and how they're going to get it, and they never get to the point of making decisions.

As a leader, how do you create an organization where data actually speeds up decision-making instead of slowing it down? If your data is bad, then you don't have what you need to make decisions. And, ultimately, that's why we have all this data—to help make decisions and drive our business forward.

The problem in many organizations, particularly large enterprises, is that the information they have is highly dispersed and disconnected. The people who own and manage the data are also disconnected. The challenge these organizations have is this: How do you bring the right information and the right people together at the right time to make the best decisions possible?

To get the right information to the right people at the right time, you need to have an architecture and a governance of data. You have a single source, so you don't have duplication or conflicting data. The next piece is to ensure the right people have access to the data. And you have to have the ability to analyze the data, understand what it's telling you, and then propose different options to get to a decision or action. The last part is the accountability. To be able to make the decisions, people have to study the data to decide if it supports the recommended course of action depending on what they were trying to accomplish. The more open and transparent you can be with data, the better.

Am I suggesting that human insights are never needed? No. Common sense, your gut feelings, intuition, whatever you call it, has its place.

There are, in fact, circumstances where our gut feelings may be *more* important when it comes to decisions. Research tells us that there are definite circumstances when we need to use our common sense over data and analytics. But sometimes you need to make decisions or try new ideas absent any data that will indicate whether they will work. You may need to step outside the expected and do something unexpected.

In 1914, Henry Ford was watching a decline in car sales coupled with high worker turnover—not an optimal state of affairs for a large automobile manufacturer. So, he did something that would have been considered irrational at the time. He doubled his employees' wages to $5 an hour. Within two years, turnover declined sharply while productivity nearly doubled, and demand for Ford cars boomed because the company's own workers could afford the cars they were making. In those two years, profits doubled from $30 million to $60 million.[27]

It was a remarkable move that no logical data would ever suggest. It was *creative*.

Where do you think the most creative ideas come from? *Humans*—not machines, which can count and analyze, but not yet generate creative ideas.

We have all experienced a data science "fail" in our personal lives. For example, you follow your GPS on your phone to nowhere or your credit card suddenly stops accepting charges because some algorithm in a faraway computer had deemed you to be a high risk.

We see it in the workplace as well—whether you are in the medical field, education system, or the technology sector. Right now, academics, economists, and entrepreneurs are grappling with the idea of autonomous cars. Will they ever be truly autonomous and not need human interaction? Someday, I'm sure, but that day might be farther away than many of us think. We are realizing that, unlike humans, self-driving cars cannot understand context. Sometimes we have to make a quick decision when there is a last-minute detour or new paint on the ground or signs to indicate danger, and autonomous cars just don't have the ability to compute all those data inputs instantly.

I believe we will always need humans in some capacity to ensure we are making the right decisions, and we will need these humans to have upstanding character to ensure the decisions are made the right way—ethically, and in keeping with the promises we have made to our customers. So, the question is what's the best way to make decisions to ensure we balance our own personal character, assumptions, and data science?

I have a suggestion.

One of the ways to get that balance is being grounded with insightful information, gathered with character. The answer is not more data or bigger data. It's about getting the right data and the right perspectives to the right people at the right time. In an ideal world, data and human intuition and character work hand in hand to lead to better decisions.

Hypergrowth Expectations

No matter what business you're in, growth is one of your most important metrics. Meeting growth expectations requires agility, speed, data, and strategy alignment. Successful organizations are priced for perfection. The pressure is enormous.

We know from Anaplan's hypergrowth experience, and from observing other highly successful businesses, that focused strategy is how we realize growth. It is essential for business strategy to encompass both character and culture—not just what we do but how we do it.

According to a report published by the U.S. Chamber of Commerce Foundation, there are three primary filters by which the public views and evaluates companies. Each of these filters relates to one another in a very powerful way:

- **Brand.** What the company says it is.
- **Reputation.** What the public thinks about the company.
- **Behavior.** How the company acts in the communities in which it serves.[28]

Character is at the intersection of these three filters, and it determines whether someone—a customer, a prospective employee, a vendor, an investor, a member of the community—will be willing to enter into a relationship of trust with a company. Without character, there is no trust; without trust, there is no business. All three of these filters must be strongly positive for your company to attract the people you need to feed hypergrowth.

Is your organization up to the challenge? Ask yourself whether you agree or disagree with these statements as an initial assessment on the health of your company character:

- Leadership has the ability to be agile and fluid.
- Important decisions are made at every level of the organization.
- Our leadership team embraces change.
- Our leaders encourage creative thinking.
- Our organization embraces change.
- Our company tends to learn from our mistakes.
- Our company has a clear vision, mission, and metrics.
- Our organization is willing to sacrifice short-term recognition for longer-term success.
- Our organization has experience with managing process change.
- Our organization understands the value of "working smarter, not harder."

I suggest that the more you disagree with these statements, the more likely that your organization is not positioned as well as it could be for hypergrowth. In fact, your organization may very well be set up for failure.

Customers First

Today, people simply do not have patience for less-than-stellar service, reliability, and quality—whether as consumers or business-to-business buyers. Customer choice rules the day, and businesses relying on loyalty today for loyalty tomorrow will be challenged. Growth depends on tight alignment of market needs and proprietary solutions. Intentional customer experience distinguishes players. Companies that ignore customer desires or dissatisfaction often don't survive—think of the legacy businesses overtaken by the sharing economy or mobile and social content. Serving customers first is a required mantra for thriving business.

But to serve customers first, leaders must also serve their people. Far too many leaders treat the members of their team like they are just a production line—not individuals who have hopes and aspirations and who want to be part of something bigger than themselves. As a leader, you can operate your organization in a way that is very mechanical, or you can operate it in a way where you provide an element of fun, camaraderie, or celebration.

You can choose to encourage people to bring the best of themselves to their work every day—putting customers at the center of everything they do—or you can choose to encourage people to see their job as "just a paycheck" with no emotional investment or passion. And I will tell you, because I've seen both types of organizations, that leaders who put a much greater emphasis on the people side of it have much better outcomes— better products, better service—and much happier customers.

Go to a business where managers spend time with their employees, where they greet their customers. If they feel good, they're going to feel good about greeting customers. They're going to go the extra step to be able to give you more attention and better service, versus a workforce that is disengaged and putting in minimum effort. The ethos of care and taking pride in one's work trickles down throughout the organization, and it impacts a company's results by impacting its customers.

In the next chapter, we dig deeper into what upstanding character means for an organization, and how building a character-led culture based on respect, trust, co-creation, and other factors all leads to higher performance.

The New Essential Core: Upstanding Character

"Watch your character, it becomes your destiny."

—*Lao Tzu*

Having a disengaged character is the same as having no character.

We all have our own definition of what character is—especially when it comes to *personal* character, the kind of character that is within each and every one of us. But I'm sure that our definitions of *character* are not all that different from one another. Generally, a definition of *personal character* will include traits such as honesty, strong values, moral excellence, integrity, compassion, and so on. Essentially, character is the code of conduct that we apply when we have choices to make—it's a framework for decision making. It's also the foundation of trust we need to build strong and lasting relationships with others.

When we talk about *company* character, I think there is a subtle, but significant, difference from the way we talk about personal character. As I mentioned earlier, companies with upstanding character embody empathy, courage, authenticity, honesty, integrity, respect, and so on—very much the kinds of things we expect people with strong personal character to embody. However, when you're talking about an organization, there's more to upstanding character than these traits. Upstanding character is informed by the values that an organization and its leadership, teams, and partners embrace and commit to that define their behavior.

I asked Yvonne Wassenaar—CEO of Puppet, a provider of software solutions that automate how its clients continuously deliver, make compliant, remediate, and manage their multi-cloud environments—for her perspective on company character. Says Wassenaar:

> I think about character in terms of three areas: what does the service or offering you're bringing represent to the market (e.g., value, durability, playfulness), what are the values of the people or teams that deliver the service or make the offering, and how do these individuals show up (e.g., what's their personality? Not just what they say, but what do they say and do in service to your customer?)? Character is a combination of all these things. And where does that character come from? I believe, at its core, the character of a company comes from the people on your team—at the end of the day, people make companies who they are.[1]

Like many other organizations, to ensure every Anaplan employee and partner is working from a shared point of view, we have published a set of values that we are all expected to live by.[2] I hold myself and our teams accountable to our values. We spotlight values stories at our Company Update meetings, and we have recognition programs to acknowledge employees who have embraced them and put them to work in their own jobs. And I personally do my best to live Anaplan values every day:

- Open;
- Authentic;
- Inclusive;
- Collaborative;
- Creative; and
- Tenacious.

Open doesn't just mean being open to new information, although that's certainly an important part of this particular value. It means being open to change, innovation, and transformation. And it means being open to feedback from others, both positive and negative. For example, if your manager suggests that improving your presentation skills would be valuable for your career development, you're able to accept the feedback and let go of what's made you successful in the past to try new approaches and strategies. Open also means communicating transparently without a hidden agenda and being willing to share information and knowledge with others rather than holding it in a silo. Being open helps to develop trust, which is the bedrock for all of the Anaplan values.

Authentic is all about bringing our real selves—our best selves—to work. We each have our own circumstances and unique history that make us who we are. It used to be that there was a hard wall between your professional identity and your personal life, but things have evolved. While we have always valued authenticity, it's even more relevant and necessary since COVID-19 forced us to work from home for an extended period of time. Being invited into people's homes for virtual meetings has been both rewarding and humbling. It's been a real lesson in empathy. I encourage everyone in Anaplan to bring their real, authentic selves to work and to do so without fear or discomfort. When we are supported and empowered to be ourselves, it really frees people to do their best work and reach their full potential.

Inclusive means welcoming everyone to the table, regardless of gender, age, sexual orientation, beliefs, ethnicity, physical ability, or any of the other things that make us who we uniquely are. It's about making room for others to be their authentic selves and embracing and valuing their differences. At Anaplan, we want our board, our executive team, and our workforce to be a reflection of our customers and the communities in which we do business. I'm convinced that having a diverse and inclusive workforce is not only desirable, it's the key to our success, now and in the future. We want the very best, most talented people—regardless of what their backgrounds might be—to come to Anaplan and build lasting careers. We need their ideas, their perspectives, and their voices. Fostering diversity and inclusion is unquestionably the right thing to do and it's also good for business. In just one example, according to a 2020 McKinsey report, companies in the top quartile for ethnic and cultural diversity were 36 percent more profitable than companies in the bottom quartile.[3]

Collaborative is more than just working together on teams or sharing ideas. It's about taking opportunities and challenges and finding the best people in the organization to work on them regardless of boundaries or hierarchy. While this might take the form of formal, cross-functional teams, it's also quite simply a recognition that good ideas can come from anywhere in the company. When we collaborate with others both in and out of the organization, we create value, which we then deliver to our customers. A key component of collaboration is sharing the work—and sharing credit too. Rather than trying to keep the spotlight on yourself, true collaboration is about elevating ideas and creating the best solutions for the good of the company and our customers, not just for individual rewards or recognition.

Creative is a willingness to look beyond existing approaches and structures when trying to solve difficult problems for ourselves or our customers. It encompasses seeing opportunities, taking risks, and pushing ourselves to innovate and advance our capabilities. Although creativity is consistently rated as one of the top attributes that employers seek when hiring, according to a Conference Board survey, 85 percent of employers said that they were having difficulty finding qualified applicants with the right characteristics.[4] In addition, according to research conducted by Adobe, 75 percent of respondents reported that they are under pressure to be productive on the job instead of creative, with only 1 in 4 employees believing that they are living up to their creative potential.[5] Even more troubling is the fact that many employees are afraid to volunteer new solutions that don't fit the organization's prevailing wisdom. It only takes one negative comment or non-response from a manager or executive to discourage an employee from being creative on the job.

Finally, *tenacious* means that we don't give up easily—we'll try every possible route to a solution and persevere until we get there. Part of the reason why we are so tenacious is that we always strive to put our customers first. We are focused on finding innovative solutions to their most difficult problems and making their planning and other systems more effective and efficient. But these solutions aren't easy—there are many moving parts, enormous data sets, and multiple stakeholders to satisfy. A tremendous amount of effort goes into making sure our customers' implementations are successful and they feel well supported every step of the way. That requires tenacity. What it doesn't mean, however, is that we expect our people to put in 12-hour days, week after week, until they collapse from burnout. Tenacity includes knowing when to pause and rest, so that you can come back with renewed energy, innovation, and applied creativity to solve problems and continue the journey.

In addition to living our values, at Anaplan, we share a common mindset. We call this approach being "A-shaped"—A as in Anaplan. A-shaped people live our values every day and get their work done in the following ways:

A-shaped people start with our customers.
A-shaped people think big and act bold.
A-shaped people win with speed and innovation.
A-shaped people act like owners.

Anaplan's values were developed in a very intentional way. First, we worked together to determine the behaviors that were already in practice throughout the organization, and then we asked employees what kind of values they considered essential in an organization they wanted to work for and that they personally aspired to and would be proud of. Then finally, I weighed in along with my executive team with the values that we felt were critically important.

It was no surprise to me that the list of values we came up with was remarkably consistent—we shared a very common perspective on how we would conduct ourselves as A-shaped people.

As I noted in the introduction, Anaplan values were instrumental to our collective performance in 2020. All the investment of time, energy, and attention to communicate, recognize, and reinforce our values created the resilience we needed to weather the cascading waves of external crises hitting employees, customers, and partners. We had built a position from which we could quickly and decisively act. In hindsight, it's clear to me how instrumental the connection between our values and culture was to our strength as a brand, a team, and a competitive force at a time when other organizations struggled.

Is Your Character Online or Offline?

When we talk about character, it's easy for us to get tangled up in the quality of the character itself. Is someone's character good or is it bad? Is it weak or strong? Is it courageous and confident, or is it hesitant and insecure?

I personally believe that the majority of people we encounter in our lives have good intentions—they want to do what's right. Sure, there are always a handful of people who let their ego or greed get in the way of doing the right thing—for example, Elizabeth Holmes of Theranos, who lied about the capabilities of her blood testing technology, and Martin Shkreli, who increased the price of toxoplasmosis/AIDS drug Daraprim from $13.50 a tablet to $750 and was convicted of defrauding investors for many millions of dollars.[6] But, in my own personal experience, these kinds of people are very much outliers.

So, let's start with the baseline assumption that the vast majority of people have decent personal character—it's part of who we are as human beings. Why then do we hear so many stories about companies and leaders that act in ways that are contrary to having upstanding character?

I asked Cy Wakeman if she could explain why some people seem to embody character, while others do not. Wakeman told me that we all have a core character but that this character can be either "online" or "offline."

When someone's character is online, it is fully activated—it is genuine and inseparable from who they are. When someone's character is offline, however, their character is not engaged; there's a gap between what they say and how they behave. Says Wakeman:

> I think we're all born inherently as really good people, and we know right from wrong. We have some inherent character within us, but our egos can push us offline, where we are unconscious or falling asleep in terms of character.[7]

People who aren't living their character are essentially sleepwalking through life—they know the right thing to do but don't do it because they have checked out and have become numb to what's happening in their surroundings. It's the difference between being very intentional about one's values or treating them as an afterthought. I wonder if this was the case for Ben Silbermann, CEO of Pinterest, who was asked to comment after the former COO of Pinterest—his No. 2 executive, whom he recently terminated—posted a highly critical blog post on Medium about gender discrimination at the company. According to Kara Swisher, writing for *The New York Times*, Silbermann reportedly oversaw "a profoundly dysfunctional culture where far too many of its roughly 2,000 employees feel left out."[8]

In a company that prides itself on empowering its customers—70 percent women[9]—to live out their aspirations, it's disturbing to hear that those who felt voiceless and left out of their culture were primarily women and people of color. This is a powerful example of an "offline" character. We explore more about the cultural disconnect at Pinterest in Chapter 7.

So, if we find that our character is offline, and we want to bring it back online, what can we do? According to Wakeman, this requires a lot of self-work:

> The only way we know is self-reflection. Instead of blaming others for your predicament, you should ask, "What can I do to lead differently?" And self-reflection is a really big component of leaders with online character. When something happens, they go first to, "What's my part in this?" "Where do I need to evolve?" "Where do I need to grow?" And then, secondly, they go to, "How can I move through the world in accordance with our values and help others?" So, they first go internal to get wisdom. And then I like to say, they move externally with the ability to really love and connect dots and bring people together. And that's really what leaders with engaged character do. They're really running a program of their own evolution.[10]

The first thing that happens to people who go offline is they quit evolving—they lose interest in being relevant for what's next. The early signs of this are either emotional avoidance or a conscious decision to stop keeping up with the times. People who are offline put up walls that separate them emotionally from the people with whom they work. So, instead of really getting to know their people and empathizing with their challenges, they avoid all that and focus strictly on results—the bottom line. When confronting problems, they assign blame externally instead of reflecting on their own accountability for what's happening.

There's also an online or offline component to what employees experience in the workplace. Wakeman explains:

> I worked with a leader who used to say to his people, "We're totally family focused. We understand that many of you have young kids. We want you to be available for your family—to be able to go to your kid's ball games or to their music recitals." I told this leader, "Stop telling people that—tell them the truth: 'We are driven on deadlines. We work hard. We play hard. There'll be times that you're here on a Sunday night 'til four in the morning. And there'll be times where you'll be able to surprise your kid during the school day in their classroom.'"[11]

This may sound counterintuitive, but wouldn't it be better to be the leader who provides realistic expectations on how and when you can put your family first? It may not always be a perfect work life blend, but being honest with clear boundaries will garner appreciation from your employees rather than appearing disconnected.

Is your character online or offline? Are you consciously living your core values or are you sleepwalking through them—unaware that you are out of alignment? If you're not sure where you're at, review the sidebar to assess your situation.

Making the decision to take your character online is the first step—and it's a big one. But you must also be accountable for the results. You must actually do what you've committed to—accountability is a mindset, not a skillset. Wakeman suggests that your readiness to be accountable has these four factors:

- **Commitment.** The willingness to do whatever it takes. Ask, "Are you in or are you out? What's your level of willingness?"
- **Resilience.** The ability to stay in. If you make a mistake, don't dwell on it. Bounce back quickly from setbacks and keep moving forward.

- **Ownership.** The ability to embrace the good, the bad, and the ugly. Recognize the positive aspects of your contributions and always invite and be open to candid and even raw feedback.
- **Continuous learning.** Mining our successes and failures for where we can grow next so we can commit to bigger things. Don't look at mistakes as failures, view them instead as teachable moments that will help you improve.[12]

As you work to take your character from offline to online, these four factors can help you get where you want to go. In fact, I consider them to be essential stepping stones.

10 Signs Your Character Is Online

We may think that our character is online, but then be surprised when we receive feedback that we're not walking our talk. Here are 10 signs that your character is online. How many of these are true for you?

1. You are intentional in your personal work to stay aligned with your company values.
2. You are attentive and tuned in.
3. You are fully engaged in your organization.
4. You're always learning.
5. You actively shape your company culture in a positive way.
6. You really care about the people who work for and with you.
7. It's about getting it done right, not just getting it done.
8. You operate skillfully and independently in the world without help from others.
9. Your energy is high.
10. You are highly visible in your organization.

10 Signs Your Character Is Offline

We're all busy people, and we may not pay attention to how our character shows up. It's therefore a good idea to periodically pause and reflect to see if you are engaging in behaviors that indicate your character is offline. Here are 10 signs that your character is offline. How many are you currently engaging in?

1. You don't do the personal work necessary to stay aligned with your company values.
2. You are checked out.
3. You are unengaged in your organization.
4. You've already learned everything there is to know.
5. You passively allow your company culture to go wherever it will go.
6. You don't really care about the people who work for and with you.
7. It's about getting it done, not getting it done right.
8. You can't operate skillfully and independently in the world without the help of others.
9. Your energy is low.
10. You try to stay under the radar as much as possible.

The DNA of Organizations with Upstanding Character

In my experience, organizations that have upstanding character have four characteristics deeply embedded in their DNA:

- **They operate with larger purpose.** Their company purpose is clear and shared. They aim to create value for all stakeholders, including employees, customers, partners, investors, and the communities in which they operate. They stand for a set of environmental, social, and governance convictions aligned with their purpose and values.
- **They are values-led.** Organizations with upstanding character have strong core values that are universally recognized, and everyone is expected to make decisions and conduct themselves through that prism. This begins with recruiting smart and talented people who are aligned with the company's values, then continues by communicating the organization's values to everyone—both inside and outside the company—continuously and in multiple channels. The ideal outcome is the values become second nature and everyone in the organization aligns with the values and lives them. People who aren't aligned with the company's values are given the opportunity to align or encouraged to find organizations that are a better fit.
- **They follow through on convictions.** Organizations with upstanding character don't just bury their values somewhere deep within their website, and then do as they please when sudden opportunities or difficult problems arise. They consistently—perhaps *obsessively*—insist

on doing what they say they are going to do. For example, a company that prides itself on being customer-centric should ensure that lines aren't long inside a store, help is easy to find, and communication channels are continually monitored so that responses are timely. The company's actions must be visibly and reliably consistent with their stated values.

- **They answer the call in challenging times.** In 2020, we faced worldwide protests against racial injustice, a global pandemic, a recession caused by the resulting business disruptions and downsizing, natural disasters, and a polarized political landscape. Any one of these events would present organizations with a tremendous challenge; all three simultaneously were unprecedented, and extremely painful for businesses and employees alike. In times like these, when confronted with a crisis, companies with upstanding character will answer the call—they make hard decisions and navigate the uncertainty guided by the values and behaviors embedded in their DNA.

Ultimately, organizations with upstanding character employ *people* with upstanding character—all the way up and down and across the organization. As I mentioned earlier, each of us has our own set of beliefs and behaviors that together form our character. However, in my own experience and research, I have found that people with upstanding character tend to have a very specific set of resonant attributes, including the following. They. . .

Have deep personal convictions. They own a deep set of core beliefs and they use these beliefs as guardrails for the decisions they make and the behaviors they engage in—or avoid. While some of these deep personal convictions may evolve gradually over time, others are held as lifelong beliefs—anchors in a world that is constantly changing.

Are authentic. They are unfailingly true to themselves and they don't hesitate to tell you what's on their minds and to give you their unvarnished opinions. You always know what kind of person you're dealing with, because authentic people know exactly what they stand for.

Are accountable. People with upstanding character hold themselves accountable for results. When they commit to completing a work product— a report, proposal, presentation, and so forth—they can be relied on to deliver. They keep their word. If for some reason they realize this will not be possible, they notify their stakeholders to work out alternatives.

When I asked Marilyn Miller—our Chief People Officer—about account-ability, she explained the interaction of personal accountability and the organization's values:

> This is uncharted territory for many companies because there used to be such separation between company values and personal perspectives. But today, we are at an entirely new level of personal account-ability. There is a newfound expectation of leaders. It is no longer enough to just manage the business. It's become important that leaders think beyond their company roles and have a personal conviction on systemic racism, environmental impact, and sustainability as well as the human side of a global pandemic or crisis. The role of leadership has evolved to include advocating and advancing solutions to these challenges that are bigger than their own business.[13]

Foster inclusivity. As research and our own experience at Anaplan show, time and time again, being inclusive leads to better outcomes for the organization. People who foster inclusivity draw others in and seek diverse thinking and experiences while upholding a shared set of values. There's plenty of research that shows the advantages of diversity and inclusion, including McKinsey's 2020 report, "Diversity Wins: How Inclusion Matters," which drew from a data set comprising more than 1,000 large businesses in 15 countries. In addition to improved profitability, the report found that companies with more diverse representation had a higher probability of outperformance. According to the report:

> Companies with more than 30 percent women executives were more likely to outperform companies where this percentage ranged from 10 to 30, and in turn these companies were more likely to outperform those with even fewer women executives, or none at all. A substantial differential likelihood of outperformance—48 percent—separates the most from the least gender-diverse companies.[14]

It's well proven that organizations do better when they recruit and nurture a diverse group of people to explore opportunities and tackle difficult problems.

Have a growth mindset. According to Stanford psychology professor Carol Dweck, those who believe that success comes from hard work, continuous learning, and persistence have a *growth mindset*—they believe that intelligence can be developed and increased and they are continuous learners.[15] Those with a growth mindset will naturally persevere despite challenges and failures—learning important lessons that eventually lead to their long-term success. They are always willing to learn more and to surround themselves with people who are more expert than they are.

Are in touch with their core value system. Our core character is forged from the beliefs that reside deepest within us. Core values influence your personal moral or ethical codes. What's most important when it comes to our core value system is whether we are actively engaged with it or disconnected and out of touch. This relates to Cy Wakeman's idea of character that can be online (activated) or offline (disengaged).

What kind of people do you have in your organization? Do they fit this profile, or do they fall short in one or more areas?

In Part II of this book, we explore the building blocks of character-driven organizations. Please keep in mind as you move forward into the next part that this is *not* a prescription—not a "check-these-boxes-and-you're-done" approach to creating a company with upstanding character. This is more food for thought—a summary of some of the things that I have personally seen during the course of my career, along with examples and insights from other business leaders.

That said, if you find your organization lacking in one or more of these six building blocks, then you might consider why it's missing, and what could be gained if it were a part of your own organization's DNA.

PART II

Building Character-Driven Organizations

CHAPTER 4

Know Your Values

"When your values are clear to you, making decisions becomes easier."
—Roy E. Disney

Upstanding character starts with defining your unique core values.

The first glass of Coca-Cola was served in Atlanta, Georgia, by Dr. John Pemberton more than 130 years ago in 1886. This was the birth of the company that came to dominate the global soft drink industry—and eventually, much more than that. Today, Coca-Cola offers its more than 500 brands—everything from Coke to Topo Chico sparkling water to Minute Maid orange juice to Honest Tea to fairlife milk—in more than 200 countries around the world.[1] I know from personal experience that you can't go anywhere overseas without encountering the iconic Coca-Cola logo—emblazoned on billboards, on the sides of buses and tuk-tuks, and in the doorways of roadside shops.

According to the Interbrand ranking of best global brands for 2020, Coca-Cola is ranked No. 6 in the world with a brand worth more than $56 billion. Only Apple, Amazon, Microsoft, Google, and Samsung are ranked higher.[2]

So, it's no surprise that when Coca-Cola's executive team and corporate communications department send out messages to the world that have the potential to affect the value of that extremely respected brand, whether in a positive or negative way, they do so only after great deliberation. Sometimes, however, events outside the company are so compelling that the company feels duty-bound to take a stance and proclaim its values.

At the time of this writing, if you visited the Coca-Cola U.S. website (https://us.coca-cola.com), in the middle of the page, in a large black box with white type, you would have found the following message:

Coca-Cola

together we must

share hope

do more

end racism

and together we will[3]

If you clicked on "Learn More" at the bottom of the black box, you would have been taken to a page that describes the company's deep commitment to its effort "to end systemic racism and bring true equality to all."[4] This commitment includes donations to 100 Black Men of America and the National CARES Mentoring Movement as well as explicit support for organizations doing work in three key areas: social justice and civil rights, women's empowerment/community empowerment, and education and youth development.

But Coca-Cola has done much more than just plaster uplifting messages across its website and social media and make some related donations. Its Chairman and CEO, James Quincey, put the company's values on full display when he updated Coca-Cola employees on "Where we stand on social justice" during a virtual town hall on June 3, 2020. While the full statement is too long to reproduce in these pages, I was particularly struck by these words:

George Floyd. Killed. A senseless tragedy for him and his family. Ahmaud Arbery. Breonna Taylor. Philando Castile. Sandra Bland. Freddie Gray. Michael Brown. Eric Garner. Tamir Rice. Trayvon Martin. All killed. All Black Americans, predominantly male Black Americans. All of whom should be alive today.

I, like you, am outraged, sad, frustrated, angry. Companies like ours must speak up as allies to the Black Lives Matter movement. We stand with those seeking justice and equality.[5]

Many companies embraced #blacklivesmatter in the wake of the killing of George Floyd by Minneapolis police in May 2020—including Apple, Walmart, Nike, Home Depot, Amazon, Levi's, and many others—issuing statements and donating to organizations fighting racial injustice. Although many corporate statements were criticized as insincere and lacking substance, for the Coca-Cola Company, this wasn't just window dressing. It was a chance to demonstrate corporate character that was remarkably consistent and stretched back several decades.

I spoke with Victor Barnes—VP/Global CFO, The McDonald's Division at The Coca-Cola Company—about his company's long history of living its values and standing up for them no matter what. Barnes talked about the true north of Coca-Cola:

> The character of the company, at its core, is about trying to be a good corporate citizen. When Martin Luther King Jr. won the Nobel Peace Prize, there were Atlanta city leaders who refused to honor Dr. King. Coca-Cola basically said, "We will move out of town if you don't do this." I think some of the company's earliest leaders had a true north that defined the fact that Coke has to be in a better place even than where society was generally. This true north is core in the company DNA.[6]

When Martin Luther King Jr. was awarded the Nobel Peace Prize in October 1964, he was the youngest person (at just 35 years old) and only the second African American and the first Georgian ever to win it. It was an event that, under normal circumstances, would have caused Atlanta's civic and business leaders to trip all over each other to be first in line to pay honor to this man who had achieved so much at such a young age. However, this was the Deep South in the 1960s, and the fact that Dr. King was Black—and not just Black, but *the* preeminent American civil rights leader—created quite a conundrum for all involved.

How to honor Dr. King?

Eventually, a small organizing group—including Atlanta Mayor Ivan Allen Jr., *Atlanta Constitution* publisher Ralph McGill, Rabbi Jacob Rothschild, and others—decided to host a banquet at Atlanta's Dinkler Plaza Hotel. A date was set, tickets were put on sale, and letters were mailed to more than 100 civic leaders, asking them to sponsor the event. After that . . . crickets. An article in the *New York Times* at the time stated, "Most of those receiving the letters have not replied, reliable sources say. A few have responded negatively, including one leading banker who strongly stated his objections."[7]

The possibility that Atlanta would throw a party for its Nobel Prize–winning hometown hero and nobody would come did not sit well with J. Paul Austin, Coca-Cola's then-chairman. At a hastily gathered meeting of Atlanta's business elite, Austin expressed his displeasure with the situation in terms that were clear and unequivocal:

> It is embarrassing for Coca-Cola to be located in a city that refuses to honor its Nobel Prize winner. We are an international business. The Coca-Cola Company does not need Atlanta. You all have to decide whether Atlanta needs the Coca-Cola Company.[8]

Reportedly, the event sold out within two hours after Coca-Cola's chairman spoke those words, with 1,500 attending the dinner in honor of Dr. King on January 27, 1965. Notably, the assembled guests joined with Dr. King at the end of the dinner to sing "We Shall Overcome"—quite a turnabout for this reluctant group of Atlanta's preeminent civic and business leaders.

After interviewing Barnes for this book, I have no doubt that Coca-Cola's chairman and executive leadership team would do exactly the same thing today. They are 100 percent committed to a culture of diversity and inclusion, with upstanding character as a constant—the North Star that guides the decisions they make.

At Anaplan, we regularly focus on our values (open, authentic, inclusive, collaborative, creative, and tenacious) as we have a global culture committee comprised of highly regarded ambassadors representing every function and from all levels and tenures in the organization. These ambassadors provide direct feedback on a regular basis on how we are living our culture, and they are the stewards of our everyday cultural activities. I consult with them often before making big decisions, such as reviewing multiple headquarters locations before we signed our lease. I wanted to make sure we included their values-based perspective of which space would offer us the most inclusivity, openness, collaboration, and creativity.

It's my fervent hope that everyone in the company takes time to consider how they can put the values to work in their lives—both on and off the job. In this chapter, we take a closer look at the ways in which organizations and the individuals who run them can identify, know, and refresh their values and set an example for others to follow.

It Starts with Personal Work

As you may recall, I introduced Jon Iwata to you in Chapter 2. In addition to his current position with the Yale School of Management, he previously served as Chairman of the Page Society, a professional association for corporate communications executives. During his time there, his organization published a report: "Corporate Character: How Leading Companies Are Defining, Activating, and Aligning Values."[9] According to this report, values are the defining elements for the expression of corporate character—they are deeply embedded in the company's DNA. Unearthing these values is therefore key to becoming a company with upstanding character. According to the report:

> The first step in developing corporate character is the clear definition of an organization's distinctive beliefs, values, and purpose—described as the value it uniquely creates for its customers, employees, and shareholders, as well as for the public at large.

Undertaking this process is increasingly necessary because greater transparency now makes it possible for anyone to see the corporation behind its products, services, and brands, and customers are increasingly likely to act on their preferences by supporting what they like and vocally opposing what they do not. Companies must therefore define values that are consistently lived out by the entire organization.

In my own experience, I have found that the first step in getting in touch with your organization's values is to first get in touch with your own values, and this starts with personal work. There are a variety of different ways you can do this exploration.

One possibility is introspection—looking deep inside yourself to find the answers you seek. This can be difficult in the heat of a busy day at the office (home or otherwise), or while you're fighting fires at work, or when you've got a thousand and one things on your mind. What works for me when I need clarity is to extract myself from all the distractions and interruptions and think about what is most important to me. I've been a runner for years, and the time I spend running is meditative and really lends itself to this kind of deep reflection. Ask yourself: What are the values that *you* hold near and dear? Which ones do you consider to be essential, values that are a personal red line for you, and which ones are more flexible? Take note of the answers to these questions and capture any other insights that might arise.

Another possibility is engaging in mindfulness practice, which I consider to be a form of introspection. *Mindfulness* can be defined simply as paying attention to the present moment without judgment. Without judging which values you *think* you are supposed to consider most important, which ones actually most resonate with you, and which ones excite you the most? However, you can extend mindfulness practice to think about the future as well, which can help you to generate future possibilities and options.

The Mayo Clinic recommends that people engage in mindfulness practice every day, and it offers a variety of simple ways to do it, including:

- Pay attention;
- Live in the moment;
- Accept yourself;
- Focus on your breathing;
- Engage in body scan meditation;
- Try sitting meditation; and
- Attempt walking meditation.[10]

We're all very busy people, and the constant change that we're currently immersed in drains us of both the time and energy to go through exercises like this. We may in fact think we just don't have room in our daily schedule to unplug—even for only a few minutes a day. However, I argue that during times like these, we need to engage in a mindfulness practice more than ever. Regardless of what time I complete my workday, I make time for myself. I go for a run, walk, or bike ride with my son around our neighborhood. I sometimes cook my famous chili or simply weed my garden and chase the rabbits away.

We need to remove ourselves from the chaos and the interruptions and the distractions, and let our minds wander where they will. Taking the time to do this gives our brains time to recharge and find new creative pathways—net positives that will make us better people, both on and off the job.

Know What You Stand For

Another way to discover what your personal values are is to take an assessment or diagnostic. A series of carefully crafted questions can help tease out the values that are important to you. Doug Merritt is President and CEO of Splunk, provider of technology used for application management, security, and compliance as well as business and web analytics. We both worked at Cisco, and I respect him as an astute businessperson and a longtime colleague. Most executives like Merritt and me have taken all sorts of assessments that are meant to tell us what kind of personality we have, our strengths and weaknesses, and much more. These assessments can also give us a pretty good idea of what we stand for. I asked Merritt to tell me how the assessments he has taken, and the feedback he has received from others, have informed his knowledge of what he stands for.

> The myriad of tests that I've done over the years—from Myers-Briggs to HBDI to Spencer Stuart, to a recent Korn Ferry 360 review—they've been very consistent for a couple of decades. According to these tests, I am very purpose- and learning-driven. Those are my two main mantras. And within purpose and learning there is a complementary focus on growth mindset—which Carol Dweck has done a great job of framing and naming and popularizing. Dweck's work provides a very clear basis for knowing what you stand for and then using that knowledge to create favorable outcomes. This has been really key to the way that I view the world and operate in the world.[11]

When Merritt took the reins of Splunk upon the retirement of his predecessor, Godfrey Sullivan, he took a considerable amount of time to determine what his own values were, how they were similar to or different from Sullivan's, and then codified them into a set of leadership principles for the company to follow. Says Merritt:

> After Godfrey retired, I waited for almost two years to come out with my own leadership principles. I really wanted to feel like I had settled into the role of CEO and ensure that anything I came out with around leadership principles—which I think of as really character or behavioral principles—was in alignment with the company. I spent a lot of time writing down, rewriting, and refining the leadership principles that I felt were both an authentic reflection of my beliefs and aligned with the Splunk culture and needs. The end result was four leadership principles that are centered around growth mindset: listening more than talking, high empathy, risk-taking, and focusing on the big rocks. It's communicated to every new hire group, it's woven through our new hire training, they're used as you advance through different managerial levels, and at the exec staff level. After I set the guideposts, our sales

enablement, learning and development teams, and operations teams rolled them out to make sure that what we were doing was going to be consistent with those beliefs.[12]

Identify Values in Partnership with Employees

While it's critical for leadership to embody a company's values, I don't believe the CEO needs to be the sole keeper or determinant of its values. Sure, I know that my own personal values have a significant influence over Anaplan's values—any company's values are a reflection of what the CEO believes and what behaviors employees are rewarded for. However, the best way for employees in every part of an organization to feel invested in its values is to involve them in their formulation.

When I walked in the door at Anaplan in 2017, the company had a published set of four values: disruption, speed, accountability, and integrity. And although the company had promoted these values internally—and marketed them externally—they were honestly not present in everyday office life as a foundation of the Anaplan culture. While it could be argued that they reflected where the company had once been, they didn't inspire or shape the company that we aspired to be in the future.

So, I decided that we needed to enlist the participation of *all* our employees to create a new set of values that would be "of the people, by the people, and for the people." It wasn't good enough to just "freshen them up." Our goal was to create values that actually fit our organization and that would help us recruit the people we wanted to work with. I knew that, to be successful, we would need to get leadership buy-in—from the executive leadership team to each of our people managers. Integrating the values into Anaplan's DNA would require that they be maintained, supported, and reinforced. If the leadership team didn't truly believe in the values we came up with, then there was no way we would be able to maintain our credibility in this effort.

We put together an action plan for creating our new set of core values, involving a broad cross-section of the organization at points in the process.

The first step was an initial research phase led by a small team, around the question: "Anaplan connectedness"—what does it mean to be connected? We gathered feedback from teams and best practices from other successful companies with strong cultures to better understand how we could best create values that reflected Anaplan's personality—something genuine we could live and breathe.

The next step was to host cultural workshops at different Anaplan locations globally over the course of three weeks. These workshops took place in San Francisco, Minneapolis, three different locations in the United Kingdom (London, York, and Maidenhead), and Singapore. We scheduled one additional session for remote employees who didn't work in these locations. Our goal for each session was to get a list of five bubbled-up values, their definitions, and a set of observable behaviors.

We next aligned the results of these workshops with our vision team—staying aligned with their progress. We knew that even though Anaplan's vision doesn't dictate its culture, it would have a direct effect on the tone and the messaging of the values that we ultimately selected as an organization. To have a cohesive message, both inside and outside the organization, we would need to closely align our vision, mission, and values.

Next, the findings and top values were presented to the executive leadership team (ELT) to get the team's feedback, consent, and approval of the values and the next steps.

While gaining the approval of the ELT might be the final step in a values exercise in some organizations, we wanted to get all our employees involved again in the process to make sure we got them right. We explained what the top values were and how they were selected, sent out a survey to get additional feedback from employees throughout the company, and then opened up a Slack channel to engage in conversation with our people. The result was a final set of values, their definitions, and observable behaviors.

Finally, we rolled out the values to the organization, and to the world at large. Employees created blog posts explaining what the new values meant to them. We knew we would need the management team's help, so we made the values and observable behaviors a part of our management and leadership training. We wanted the values and behaviors to be a part of our managers' vocabulary as they trained and coached their teams. In addition, we tied the values to our quarterly recognition program and to our recruitment efforts.

In this way, we created a new set of Anaplan core values—along with definitions and observable behaviors—in an inclusive way that involved every employee. We then fostered adoption of the values through vocabulary, visibility, and recognition programs, and we measured the engagement of the company and support of the new values through the number of participants at culture workshops, membership in the Slack channel, and total survey takers.

I believe that the values we came up with very accurately reflect who we are as Anaplan, and they have a direct influence on the uniquely powerful culture that we have created. The process took longer than if we had done just a simple update, but the outcome was well worth it. About 70 percent of our employees worldwide voluntarily participated, and our people have embraced these values. That said, I know we're not perfect and we can never be satisfied with the status quo. We're always trying new things, learning, exploring, and finding innovative ways to deliver greater value to our customers—using upstanding culture as our foundation and our North Star.

Five-Step Values Workshop Process

Getting employees to come up with their suggestions for meaningful core values required that we have a well-defined process of workshops, which we rolled out globally over a three-week period. Please note that this process takes a lot of time and you need exceptional facilitators (we already had some in-house experts who were up for the challenge). But I will tell you from experience that it's well worth the time and engagement that follows when you get your own passionate, eager employees involved. Here's the five-step process that we used. The workflow can be adapted for virtual teams using digital collaboration tools.

Step 1—The Core Values List Question

To create your own core values list you start with this question:

"What is important at our company and what is unique about working here?"

The exercise works best if the question is visible to you throughout the rest of the exercise. You can:

- Print the question and place it on the table in front of you.
- Write the question on a whiteboard.

Step 2—Creating the Core Values List

Take 10 minutes to answer this question. Write down every answer that comes to mind, putting each idea on its own separate index card or Post-it Note®. You can stop writing ideas when your 10 minutes are up or when your index cards are full. These cards are your core values list. Display the cards randomly so every idea is visible.

For the exercise to work well, you should have a minimum of 20–25 ideas written down on your cards before moving on. If your idea flow slows, try inverting the question. Ask yourself, "What is our company NOT?" or "What do similar companies do that our organization would never do?" Inverting the question often helps come up with a fresh group of ideas.

Step 3—Organizing Your Core Values List

Now you are ready to organize your core values list. Instead of picking cards at random that sound good to you, begin to sort the cards into 5–7 groups that feature similar ideas. This process is commonly referred to as *affinity mapping* or creating an *affinity diagram*. Affinity mapping helps you find patterns in a large set of data by identifying underlying relationships.

For example, if you wrote down "Teamwork" on one card and "Good Communication" on another card, you may decide those two ideas are similar and should be grouped together. Here are a couple of thoughts to help with sorting your core values list:

- Make sure every card remains visible throughout the sorting process, so you can be flexible as you notice new relationships.
- Move ideas (cards) that don't have a place into a "parking lot" on the side of your sorting area. Come back to the parking lot later in the sorting process to see if these ideas now have a place.
- Do not discard any ideas even if they are repeated. Repetition is a signal of importance or shared thinking if you created the core values list with multiple people from your management team.

Step 4—Selecting Your Core Values

Now you are ready to choose your core values from your organized core values list. Look at each of the 5–7 groups you created. Choose a key word or concept that summarizes each group of cards. This is where a large list of core values can actually come in handy. Viewing a large list of ideas can help you capture the right words to summarize each of your groups.

The key word or concept you chose from each group is one of your core values. The core values you have selected will be amazingly accurate because each group of ideas is weighted by significance (the number of cards) and is made up of everything you identified as most important or unique about your organization.

> **Step 5—Defining Your Core Values**
>
> You can easily come up with the definitions for your core values using the ideas found in each group of cards. Look for key concepts that appear on multiple cards within a group. The definitions should use the terminology found on the actual cards as much as possible. It will be easier to communicate your core values when their definitions are in your own words and understood by everyone in the organization.

Involving employees in developing your values is a great way to get buy-in. When I spoke with Sara Park—Vice President, Integrated Planning at The Coca-Cola Company—she had an interesting perspective. Says Park about a previous employer:

> I worked at a company where my values did not align with the company ownership values. I was there only for a short time, but it was incredibly difficult to show up to work as my entire authentic self, because I couldn't be open. The company wasn't seeking external perspectives or points of view, and I felt that was a huge weakness, because in a very hyper-connected and fast-changing environment, if you are static and you're not getting that external perspective, then you become a dinosaur. You're not evolving together. So, at the first chance, I left.[13]

This all changed for Park when she went to work for Coca-Cola. She explains:

> I'm very fortunate because when I talk about a positive culture, I am experiencing it right now. I love my job and I love the work that I do. I love the leadership that I work for and the team that I lead. And, I have really thought hard about why do I love that so much? It's because we are allowed to be agile. We are encouraged to be intellectually curious. We are asked to be inclusive and diverse. Our voices are heard. We are no longer asking for perfection on day one—we are really living by the principle that we can be iterative and continuously learn and improve. To be honest, my success at Coca-Cola over the last three years resulted from this cultural shift within the company.

In some organizations, defining values is an iterative and inclusive process that allows for a wide variety of input. Making sure everyone's voice is heard can be a significant undertaking, but it can be broken down into five elements:

- **Start at the top.** For a values exercise to succeed over the long term, it must have the explicit and ongoing support of a company's CEO. Again, while the CEO is not the only steward of an organization's values, this position will have a tremendous influence on them. Be sure that you have CEO buy-in for your process of specifying values before you get too far down the road. Otherwise, the process is unlikely to achieve traction and adoption.
- **Get employees involved in the process.** While codifying an organization's values most often starts at the top, that's definitely not where it ends. There are a number of great reasons for involving every employee—from the CEO and executive team (and even the board) to front-line employees—in the process. First, you'll likely get ideas that you had never thought of. Second, when employees have a voice in specifying the values that are going to guide their work lives, then they will be much more supportive of them. Finally, involving every employee in the process helps you communicate the values across and up and down the organization.
- **Choose values that resonate inside *and* outside the organization.** Your company's values need to support two distinct constituencies— your employees inside the organization and your stakeholders outside the organization. Some values, such as "honesty" or "innovation," have impact both inside and outside the organization. However, some—such as "customer success"—may have direct impact only *outside* the company. Ideally, the values you come up with should be meaningful on both sides of your company walls.
- **Values should be enduring, but be prepared for updates.** We've previously discussed Anaplan's values: open, authentic, inclusive, collaborative, creative, and tenacious—which are key to everything we do in this company. It's what we fondly call #AnaplanLOVE (Living Our Values Everyday). When I look at those values right now, it's hard for me to imagine that any of them should change. They are generally expected to endure, but some will not stand the test of time and may need to be updated as our business environment changes. For example, the sixth Anaplan core value, *tenacious*, was added later because we

wanted a core value that was more action-oriented and reflected the urgency we feel in getting our solutions in the hands of customers around the world as quickly as possible. So, in this case, we were open to updating our values to evolve with where we were as a company.

■ **Communicate your values widely, and often.** Once you've got your values, you need to communicate them to everyone consistently and via multiple channels. Share them with employees in all-hands and team meetings, publish them prominently on your intranet and website; use them when you're recruiting new employees; incorporate them into other company programs (benefits, recognition, learning and development, etc.); talk them up with customers, partners, and vendors; and take every opportunity to tell stories about how employees live up to the values and bring them to life. And above all, make sure that you embrace these values and live them yourself. When you do that, you communicate to all around you that they are important to you, that these values really matter, and they will follow your lead.

While there are many other approaches available to you when it comes to specifying your values, the main thing to remember is that the process should be an inclusive one. It may start at the top, but if you involve others in the organization to help, there's a much better chance that the values will be embraced by all.

Review and Update Your Values

While the Page Society report I referred to earlier in this chapter is chock-full of information about the interplay of corporate character and values, I would like to focus on one key aspect of it: the process of reviewing and updating your values. Unless you are leading a brand-new startup, chances are your organization already has a set of values, and your work will not revolve around creating them from scratch, but rather revising and evolving them to align with a change in the company or culture.

This process is best described by reviewing the first three findings from the executive summary of the report based on Page's research conducted with 25 Fortune 50 companies.

Finding 1: The vast majority of the companies interviewed were actively examining and defining values. According to the report, every one of the 25 companies interviewed was focused on values, with 24 of the companies either currently in the process of reviewing or revising their values, or that were recently in the process. In the case of General Electric (GE), this took the form of reviewing the company's statement of corporate purpose ("to invent and build things that matter"), and in the case of Kroger and Cardinal Health, to create new or updated values statements that highlighted the central role of serving customers. After emerging from bankruptcy, a new statement of values created by General Motors served as "an important element in the process of stabilizing the business and giving employees a sense of direction for the company."

Finding 2: Organizations did not undertake changes in their values lightly, and the level of definition or redefinition varied widely. Overall, most of the Fortune 50 companies interviewed did not engage in a complete redefinition of their values since these values were often "deeply ingrained in the organization's identity and culture." In the cases when changes to values *were* extensive, this was most often the result of a major transition, such as a crisis or arrival of a new CEO. According to the report, Page's research revealed four levels of values definition or redefinition:

- **Refreshing, modernization, or revival of long-held principles.** In many cases, this approach led to a values statement that was shorter and more action oriented. Archer Daniel Midlands (ADM) transformed its code of conduct (titled the ADM Way) into a set of corporate values, while Cardinal Health refreshed its values with the aim of making them more conversational—hopefully, engaging employees in a dialogue about them.

- **Gradual evolution over time.** As I mentioned earlier, after we created a new set of values for Anaplan, we realized the need to add an additional one: *tenacious*. This represented an evolution of the ones we had selected in our values exercise as well as a further evolution of the ones that were already in place when I arrived in 2017.

- **Affirmation or even revival of previously held values.** When a new CEO at Home Depot reviewed the company's values, he discovered that the "values wheel" and "inverted pyramid"—values-related diagrams that dated to the company's founding, but which had been set aside by his predecessor—were so popular with employees that he immediately restored them.

- **Largely or entirely new statements of values.** When a new CEO committed to changing the company's values and culture arrived at

Ford, the company created an entirely new values statement. And when a new CEO arrived at IBM, the company took a fresh look at its Basic Beliefs values statement—introduced in 1962 and described in the Introduction—reaching out to tens of thousands of employees worldwide for their suggestions. When Verizon developed its "We are Verizon" credo, the emphasis was on focusing it outward to the customer instead of inward to employees.

Finding 3: Redefining values starts at the top with the CEO and other C-suite executives, and often includes significant employee and stakeholder input. So, while the CEO is crucial to any effort at redefining a company's values, others—including other C-suite executives—must also play key roles. Page's research found that the process of redefining values usually took place in one of four ways:

- **A "solo act" involving values crafted completely by the CEO.** For example, informal expressions of values at JPMorgan Chase were directly attributable to the actions and statements of the CEO and the people directly reporting to him. These values were then rolled out to the organization. Ford's values statement "ONE FORD: One Team, One Plan, One Goal" was initiated by the company's new CEO, who drove the process of redefining Ford's values.

- **An "ensemble" approach led by the CEO or the CEO's designee.** While this is still a top-down approach, it enlists the leadership of other senior managers. GE's CEO initiated a review of the company's values statement, led by GE's vice president of executive development and chief learning officer and involving more than 30 senior executives who were sent to gather ideas from 100 organizations around the world. At AT&T, a group of senior managers from different parts of the organization were assigned to the Employee Engagement Advisory Board, which took on the task of redefining the company's values.

- **A "chorus" approach that is bottom-up in nature—giving employees or employee groups a major role in the process.** This process begins with input gathered from employees all across an organization. Kraft's communications team put together a six-week online chat, drawing thousands of employees—from line workers to the CEO—into the process of redefining the company's values. Kroger's process of redefining its values used an employee survey to solicit inputs as well as seeking feedback from employee culture councils.

- **An "oratorio" process that was a combination of the ensemble and chorus approaches.** This was considered to be the optimal approach with management leading but seeking broad participation from employees or representative groups. At IBM, a cross-functional task force created an initial draft of the company's new set of values, which were then tested with approximately 1,000 employees by way of focus groups. The company then conducted a "ValuesJam," where it used IBM's intranet to solicit ideas from tens of thousands of employees.

When we at Anaplan periodically review our own values, we generally embark on an oratorio process that is both top down *and* bottom up. I personally believe this gets us to the best answer—merging together the values that the executive team and I hold near and dear, along with the values that our front-line employees have found to be important in their own work lives as they interact with our customers, partners, vendors, and other stakeholders. I share more about our top-down, bottom-up approach in the next chapter.

Regardless of which approach you choose, the simple fact is that you can't afford to let your values remain frozen in time—posted in a picture frame on the wall, buried somewhere in your company website, or embedded in a presentation to new hires never to be seen again. While an organization's deepest values will likely change little over time, the world is constantly changing all around us, and it would be shortsighted for our values not to keep up with those changes. The best leaders make time for this important exercise. In the next chapter, we consider how values evolve and how to best communicate them—both inside and outside the organization.

CHAPTER 5

Top Down, Bottom Up

"We're all under the same sky and walk the same earth; we're alive together during the same moment."

—*Maxine Hong Kingston*

Authentic company values come from an ongoing dialogue, constant vigilance, and recognition of exemplary behavior.

So, where does a company's character—and ultimately, its values and culture—come from? Do these things reflect the fundamental beliefs and actions of a CEO, or do they bubble up from front-line employees, collectively becoming the organization's culture and way of doing things? Or are they a combination of both—meeting somewhere in the middle?

In my experience, it's the CEO who initially lays down the various aspects of a company's character and the values that guide decision-making, hiring, firing, and other business considerations. These then evolve over time—sometimes with the arrival of a new CEO, or with input from employees throughout the organization, or smaller groups such as the executive team or a select cross-functional team. But even as a company's culture and core values evolve, the CEO often still exerts tremendous influence over them, in some cases, long after they have left the organization.

A.G. Lafley, former Chairman, President, and CEO of Procter & Gamble (P&G), agrees with this assessment. He tells the story about when he met with management guru Peter Drucker and a group of CEOs and management scholars who met to answer this question: What is the work of the CEO? During the course of this meeting, Drucker explained that there are four fundamental tasks that are the unique province of CEOs. The fourth of these tasks is *shaping the values and standards of the organization*. Said Drucker about this vital task, "CEOs set the values, the standards, the ethics of the organization. They either lead or they mislead."[1]

Lafley relates this to his own experience when he became Procter & Gamble's CEO. To give you a little background, A.G. Lafley served as CEO twice. He was first named CEO in June 2000. At the time, Procter & Gamble was a company in deep crisis. P&G had announced in March 2000 that it would miss its projected third-quarter earnings, and the company's stock price plunged from $86 to $60 in just one day, dragging down the entire Dow Jones Industrial Average along with it.[2]

Lafley knew that for Procter & Gamble's employees to regain their confidence and feel good again about their future prospects, he would have to come up with a plan to recover that was aligned to the company's core values and culture. Creating this plan was Lafley's highest priority after he became CEO. Lafley explains the challenge he faced in shaping P&G's values and standards:

> The challenge was to understand and embrace the values that had guided P&G over generations—trust, integrity, ownership, leadership, and a passion for winning—while reorienting them toward the outside and translating them for current and future relevance.[3]

In an article published by *Harvard Business Review*, James Collins and Jerry Porras explained, "Companies that enjoy enduring success have core values and a core purpose that remain fixed while their business strategies and practices endlessly adapt to a changing world."[4] This dynamic of preserving the core while stimulating progress was key to Lafley's success at Procter & Gamble.

When he took the reins as CEO in 2000, the company's market cap was in the range of $50–60 billion. Over the years, while the business strategy evolved, the focus on core values remained rock solid. When Lafley stepped down as CEO almost 10 years later—turning the reins over to new CEO Robert McDonald—Procter & Gamble's market cap had grown to $160 billion. He was hailed as one of the truly great CEOs in the history of American business.[5]

Unfortunately for P&G, the fast-moving, innovative culture that Lafley had championed while he was CEO started to slow after his departure. Critics pointed out that data-driven McDonald lagged when it came to developing new products, cutting prices on existing products in response to the 2008 economic downturn, and finding much-needed cost savings in the organization.[6] Profits and share price suffered, and P&G began to fall behind its rivals.

McDonald became the target of criticism by former P&G executives and one of the company's top shareholders, hedge fund manager Bill Ackman, who said that he was distracted from his focus on solving P&G's woes because he served on too many corporate boards. According to Ackman's calculations, this took up 25 percent of McDonald's time.[7]

McDonald eventually stepped down as CEO, and in May 2013, Lafley rejoined P&G as CEO for a second time—reinstating the culture he'd previously presided over. Soon after returning to the helm, Lafley cut costs and unveiled a plan to sell off or pull the plug on more than half of the company's brands, which at the time included everything from toilet paper to electric razors to pet food to detergent. This was consistent with the culture he championed—both the first and the second time he served as CEO. After streamlining the fast-moving consumer goods giant, he stepped down as CEO again in November 2015—retaining the position of P&G's executive chairman until he retired in July 2016.[8]

When I talked with Laura Desmond, founder and CEO of Eagle Vista Partners, about her perspective on Procter & Gamble's difficulties, she told me that CEOs have a real challenge when it comes to driving change throughout a large organization like P&G. Says Desmond:

> There's often a disconnect between the CEO in terms of the vision, the culture, the focus, and then what I call the big fat middle of a company—the middle managers—which just isn't keeping pace with how the company is changing.
>
> I really saw P&G struggle with this after the Great Recession that started in 2008. The company's leadership knew the organization needed to change—it needed to become more agile, more nimble, more entrepreneurial. They took a ton of actions, including divesting some of the brands, reducing headcount, closing headquarters around the world, and moving regional offices.
>
> They kind of went through the standard playbook, if you will, but still had trouble moving that big fat middle because the big fat middle didn't see how the change that the senior leadership was driving actually impacted what they were supposed to do in terms of the change they were supposed to enact. And so, P&G struggled for the next decade.[9]

Collins and Porras described what they call a company's *core ideology*—what the company stands for and why it exists. They say it's "a consistent identity that transcends product or market life cycles, technological breakthroughs, management fads, and individual leaders. In fact, the most lasting and significant contribution of those who build visionary companies is the core ideology."[10]

I consider what the company stands for to be the essence of upstanding character. And what the company stands for is very much the result of what behaviors its leaders model, promote, and reward.

In Chapter 1, I discuss Uber's challenging culture, and cofounder and then-CEO Travis Kalanick's role in creating it. Under Kalanick, Uber had 14 core values, but as the author of one article pointed out, they "were almost designed to bring out the worst in people, pushing a meritocracy that valued bright ideas and aggressive growth over all else."[11]

According to Kalanick, he personally spent hundreds of hours defining this "philosophy of work" with Uber's Chief Product Officer (and former Amazon executive) Jeff Holden. Kalanick then personally presented the 14 core values to 5,000 Uber employees during a four-day, company-paid retreat in 2015.[12] The values were top-down, and clearly bore Kalanick's personal stamp.

Brad Stone—author of *The Upstarts*—interviewed numerous Uber employees to re-create a list of those company core values (followed by his own commentary in parentheses):

- **Customer obsession** (Start with what is best for the customer.)
- **Make magic** (Seek breakthroughs that will stand the test of time.)
- **Big bold bets** (Take risks and plant seeds that are 5 to 10 years out.)
- **Inside out** (Find the gap between popular perception and reality.)
- **Champion's mindset** (Put everything you have on the field to overcome adversity and get Uber over the finish line.)
- **Optimistic leadership** (Be inspiring.)
- **Super-pumped** (Ryan Graves's original Twitter proclamation after Kalanick replaced him as CEO; the world is a puzzle to be solved with enthusiasm.)
- **Be an owner, not a renter** (Revolutions are won by true believers.)
- **Meritocracy and toe-stepping** (The best idea always wins. Don't sacrifice truth for social cohesion and don't hesitate to challenge the boss.)
- **Let builders build** (People must be empowered to build things.)
- **Always be hustlin'** (Get more done with less, working longer, harder, and smarter, not just two out of three.)

- **Celebrate cities** (Everything we do is to make cities better.)
- **Be yourself** (Each of us should be authentic.)
- **Principled confrontation** (Sometimes the world and institutions need to change in order for the future to be ushered in.)[13]

According to current Uber CEO Dara Khosrowshahi, after he took over in September 2017, he spent his first two months on the job "meeting our teams around the world, dealing with a few firefights, and experiencing firsthand the entrepreneurial culture that Uber is known for." This entrepreneurial culture that Khosrowshahi experienced was still hypercompetitive, and no longer appropriate for a company that had scaled from a small startup to more than 22,000 employees globally.[14] Soon after, Khosrowshahi put his own stamp on the company culture by laying out Uber's new cultural norms in a post published on LinkedIn in November 2017.

However, instead of the top-down approach that Kalanick employed when authoring his own list of 14 core values, Khosrowshahi took a radically different, bottom-up approach. As he explained in his post:

> I feel strongly that culture needs to be written from the bottom up. A culture that's pushed from the top down doesn't work, because people don't believe in it. So instead of penning new values in a closed room, we asked our employees for their ideas. More than 1,200 of them sent in submissions that were voted on more than 22,000 times. We also held more than 20 focus groups with representatives from our Employee Resource Groups and our international offices.[15]

The result of this crowdsourcing effort was a list of eight Uber cultural norms that, according to Khosrowshahi, "came from the bottom up, so employees can feel invested and committed to them, rather than having to follow strict directives from the top."[16] These new Uber cultural norms are:

- **We build globally; we live locally.** We harness the power and scale of our global operations to deeply connect with the cities, communities, drivers, and riders that we serve, every day.
- **We are customer-obsessed.** We work tirelessly to earn our customers' trust and business by solving their problems, maximizing their earnings or lowering their costs. We surprise and delight them. We make short-term sacrifices for a lifetime of loyalty.

- **We celebrate differences.** We stand apart from the average. We ensure people of diverse backgrounds feel welcome. We encourage different opinions and approaches to be heard, and then we come together and build.
- **We do the right thing.** Period.
- **We act like owners.** We seek out problems and we solve them. We help each other and those who matter to us. We have a bias for action and accountability. We finish what we start and we build Uber to last. And when we make mistakes, we'll own up to them.
- **We persevere.** We believe in the power of grit. We don't seek the easy path. We look for the toughest challenges and we push. Our collective resilience is our secret weapon.
- **We value ideas over hierarchy.** We believe that the best ideas can come from anywhere, both inside and outside our company. Our job is to seek out those ideas, to shape and improve them through candid debate, and to take them from concept to action.
- **We make big bold bets.** Sometimes we fail, but failure makes us smarter. We get back up, we make the next bet, and we go![17]

It's too soon to tell if Khosrowshahi's new culture has successfully taken hold and transformed the company from the inside out. A profile published several months later in *WIRED* painted Khosrowshahi as mature and thoughtful compared to Kalanick's brash overconfidence ("move-slow-test-things" was embedded in the article's URL, a wink at Facebook's credo to "move fast and break things").[18] Although COVID-19 had a catastrophic impact on its core ridesharing business, it remains to be seen whether Khosrowshahi's Uber will escape Kalanick's long shadow and be remembered for its positive contributions to the world.

We know from Anaplan's hypergrowth experience and from observing other highly successful businesses that focused strategy and reliable execution are how we realize growth. Positive corporate culture—rooted by intentional character—is an enabler and accelerant to sustain that performance.

In its 2019 Employment Trends Engagement Report, research firm Quantum Workplace compiled employee surveys from more than 45 Best Places to Work contests, representing more than 600,000 employees at more than 10,000 organizations across America. The Quantum Workplace survey identified eight key culture-related drivers of employee engagement that have the greatest impact. These include:

- My job allows me to utilize my strengths.
- I trust the senior leadership team to lead the company to future success.

- I believe this organization will be successful in the future.
- The leaders of the organization value people as their most important resource.
- If I contribute to the organization's success, I know I will be recognized.
- I find my job interesting and challenging.
- I see professional growth and career development opportunities for myself in this organization.
- My opinions seem to count at work.[19]

Note that the organization's leaders play an important role in ensuring that all eight of these culture-related drivers of employee engagement are in place. Leaders ensure that their people fit the jobs they are assigned to do and they build trust with the people who work for them. Leaders are optimistic about the company's future prospects and they know how valuable their people are in attaining that future. They recognize and reward employee contributions to the organization's success and they give employees meaningful work, authority, and responsibility. Leaders help guide their employees' professional growth and career development and they make sure their people have a voice that is heard.

Clearly, core values help to shape a company's culture. Every company has values they live by whether or not they have developed an official list that is communicated to any degree. Some companies have values and cultures that are entirely different from what they say they do—they don't walk their talk. Not only must leaders intentionally develop values and communicate them, they need to gauge the degree to which the values have credibility internally and externally. And this gauging of credibility is key to engaged, online upstanding company character.

The best core values are arrived at iteratively, through an ongoing dialogue among the company's CEO, its executive team, and its employees. Your people are more likely to embrace and support them when they have a voice in defining what they are. As I describe in Chapter 4, the new set of company values we came up with after I arrived at Anaplan in 2017 was very much a top-down *and* bottom-up process. We involved everyone from our frontline employees to managers—all around the globe—in the process. As you work with your people to capture your core values, make sure:

- They reflect your unique company culture.
- They are actionable.
- They are distinctive and memorable.
- There aren't too many of them.

- They aren't just platitudes.
- They support your customers and employees.
- They are measurable.
- That employee performance reviews are tied to them.
- You are passionate about them.

As you reach out to your executive team, managers, and employees for input and feedback on your core values, keep in mind that some may never change while others may evolve over the years. Which of your core values reflect the essence of what your company believes in? Which ones need to be refined, updated, or abandoned altogether? Which ones are missing?

Eras Identify Their Leaders

Geoffrey Moore is a consultant who focuses on the market dynamics of disruptive innovations and the author of the groundbreaking book *Crossing the Chasm*. In this book, Moore provides readers with insights on how to bring cutting-edge products to progressively larger markets—making the leap in marketing and selling disruptive products to mainstream customers.

I recently asked him about the interaction of leaders and the cultures of the companies they lead. According to Moore, leaders are uniquely suited to the times in which they exist, and so different CEO personalities tend to dominate depending on what it takes to "win the game." He explains:

> In the 1990s, it was clear that a really competitive, sales-oriented CEO was the key to the game. So that was John Chambers, that was Larry Ellison, that was Bill Gates and Steve Ballmer together, and that was Michael Dell. They were all incredibly competitive, sales-oriented leaders.
>
> It's pretty clear that that's not the key to the game today. Today's CEOs are oriented around customer success and collaboration. The era kind of selects its leaders as much as the leader selects what kind of leader they'll be. And so, there's a little bit of luck or timing or whatever you would call it involved. But I would say that a good leader can move with the world, but they can't move off their center.[20]

Consider, once again, the tale of two Uber CEOs: Travis Kalanick and Dara Khosrowshahi. While Kalanick's approach did not scale with the company he cofounded, leading to his ouster under pressure from investors, the fact is that he and his team were able to build a company that completely disrupted the transportation industry and grew at a remarkably fast rate. Uber went from obscurity to becoming the highest valued private startup company in the world, a tremendous accomplishment.[21]

Was Kalanick's win-at-all-costs attitude instrumental in building the company's success? Definitely. Did his approach to doing business—and the culture he created and reinforced at the company—plant the seeds for his ultimate demise and for the company's many difficulties, some that remain even today? Without a doubt. So, while we can debate whether Kalanick was the right leader for Uber during its period of tremendous growth, Kalanick was the leader the company had. And it succeeded in spite of its leadership challenges.

But regardless of this success, there were externally visible indicators that something was not right internally. Resetting Uber's culture and trajectory would require an entirely different CEO to emerge, one who could create an organization that was more customer-centric, values-led, collaborative, and inclusive. And that CEO was Dara Khosrowshahi.

But reshaping a deeply embedded culture is no easy task, as Khosrowshahi will readily admit. In an interview one year after he left a comfortable position at the helm of Expedia to become CEO of a company that was in disarray, he explained, "If there's one area that I would have liked to change faster, it is to execute more fully on our cultural transformation as a company internally, across all levels of the company."

Khosrowshahi continued, "It's been filled with good days and bad days. The good news is that the good days are outnumbering the bad days more recently. But I didn't get into this expecting an easy ride. It's been just as challenging as I expected."[22]

Leader-led values that are contrary to an upstanding ethos will cause turbulence within an organization well before there are external indicators. Don't let that gap between your talk of good values and actual behavior go on so long that even outsiders can see a clear disconnect. Your reputation casts a long shadow, whether it's a good reputation or a bad one.

Uber has a new CEO for a new era. Years from now, we'll know for certain if he was the *right* CEO for the times.

Communicate, Communicate, Communicate

Every CEO knows the critical importance of communication to the success of the organization, and I'm no different. But I haven't always been comfortable being that person doing the communicating while standing on a stage in front of 1,000 people with a spotlight shining in my face. In fact, I've always been an introvert, which probably isn't a big surprise given my finance background. Being an introvert in leadership hasn't been easy for me, but as I became more comfortable being so much more open to input, and meeting and working with people with different views and perspectives, this helped me become a better communicator.

As I mentioned earlier, I came from a small town in upstate New York, which was very isolated and didn't have a lot of diversity. I wasn't aware of much of the world outside of that little town. When I attended college at Fordham in New York City, I experienced for the first time just how diverse the world is—the many different kinds of people who lived and worked and went to school in that great city. As I experienced more, learned more, interacted more, and engaged more with others who weren't like me, my communication changed too. My hard shell of introversion began to crack just a bit as I became more comfortable communicating with others.

We invited best-selling author Susan Cain to speak at Anaplan, and she came and talked about her book *Quiet: The Power of Introverts in a World That Can't Stop Talking*. We had a conversation on stage that has stayed with me since we talked. She was explaining that introverts are always going to be introverts, but they learn traits of extroverts in order to survive—these people are called *ambiverts*. I really resonated with this because I am much more comfortable being an introvert in most any kind of environment or situation, even though my job requires me to be an extrovert.

Prior to Cisco, I learned that you can be successful in the finance world as an introvert by not engaging much with communication and just dealing with what you have around you. When I went to Cisco, I worked closely with John Chambers—a tremendous extrovert—and I was able to understand and appreciate communication more. He held us accountable for being communicators—as leaders within the organization, but also outside the organization, engaging and interacting with customers, partners, and others.

He had a ranking mechanism with two sets of scores: executive sponsorships of customers (which measured who was active with customers) and communications. All the scores were shared within the leadership team on a regular basis. If you scored well, you got a lot of accolades—primarily from the other leaders. And if you didn't, you were pushed to improve.

At first, I thought, I'm okay with being low on the list because that's not my job as CFO. But then I realized all these other people were able to connect with our employees and get them to take action on what needed to be done. I decided to get a coach and started to learn some of the techniques of being a better communicator. With a lot of practice, hard work, and the ability to receive some raw feedback, I was able to make the top leaderboard and get recognized for the engagement we had with the customers where I was the executive sponsor.

What helped me the most was getting over the fear in my head that I was going to say the wrong thing. The only way to overcome that discomfort is to have positive experiences. Start small with safe groups or teams of people you know and trust, get some acknowledgment back, and learn from it—see how you can do it better the next time.

My other secret is, I sought feedback constantly. When I was at Cisco, I would ask the best speakers, communicators, and my peers for honest feedback. Today, at Anaplan, I constantly seek feedback. I always want to improve. I make a point of going to my trusted sources who will tell me the honest, unvarnished truth. At times, I have received cringe-worthy feedback where I instantly wanted to defend myself. But I paused because those who gave me this feedback cared enough to tell me. I thanked them and I did my best to improve for the next time.

There's one more strategy that has helped almost as much: preparing thoughtfully for every communication opportunity. I'll read through briefings before meetings, I'll make notes of ideas I want to cover in calls or conferences. Even if it's just an informal, 20-minute talk, I'll take time to prepare. A cornerstone of my prep routine is to understand as much as I can about the audience—it's an empathetic approach that helps me genuinely connect with people whether in person or virtually. I've found people appreciate the humility and authenticity conveyed. This is the through-line of my practice as a leader: applying my intention and then always improving and raising the bar.

I personally invested my time in becoming a better communicator, but it's also crucially important to have a good communication infrastructure in your organization. In any business—large, small, or in between—there is a constant stream of messages and information and data that needs to flow up, down, and sideways through the company. In many organizations, however, communication doesn't work as well as it should. Why not? Sometimes it's structural; a company's systems may not be well suited to getting messages to their intended recipients quickly and efficiently. Oftentimes it's volume; employees may be overloaded with information and have trouble prioritizing what is most important. In other cases, the problem isn't the communication per se—it's the messenger, often the frontline managers.

The results of an Interact survey conducted by Harris Poll found that a surprising 69 percent of managers reported that they are often uncomfortable communicating with employees. And, when it comes to giving direct feedback on employee performance, 37 percent of managers said that they would be uncomfortable giving that feedback if they thought their employee might respond negatively to it.[23] That is a very real problem.

When Google conducted internal research on whether managers were necessary—based on manager performance ratings and manager feedback gathered from the company's annual employee survey—the company found that managers *do* matter. In fact, Google found that employees on teams with great managers were happier and more productive than employees who worked on teams that did not have great managers.

So, Google, of course, took the next step—doing more research to reveal the behaviors that make someone a *great* manager. The company discovered 10 behaviors that high-scoring managers share, including one specific to communication: "Is a good communicator—listens and shares information."[24]

I think everyone wants more communication in their organization, not less. And it's up to us as leaders to build systems that enable and facilitate quality communication quickly, all across the organization. I believe it's also up to us as managers to initiate communication with our people and to listen—really listen—to what they have to say.

At Anaplan, we try hard to strike a balance between electronic communication efficiency and authentic interaction. And we see communication as much more than a way for the company to disseminate information to employees—we use it for recognition, feedback, sharing and collaboration, and storytelling in service to our culture and our customers. And based on the feedback we've received, our employees appreciate the effort. We always have room to improve, and that's part of the journey.

Before I arrived at Anaplan, internal communications were infrequent—there was a company meeting once a year and very few company-wide email messages. When I arrived, establishing better communication channels was something I invested in right away. We created an internal communications platform called The Barn (because our company was started in a barn in the United Kingdom, we have used that origin as a symbol of our heritage), which is our global intranet for all employees. Over the last few years, we've established quarterly company updates, CEO chats, town halls, and frequent emails about new people joining, promotions, and recognition. Having fun is also integral to our culture—we do annual lip-sync battles, parody sketches, and movie tribute videos (in my experi-ence, there's tremendous humility in donning a superhero costume in front of a crowd or dancing in a music video).

All this communication has had a major positive impact on our culture—it's strengthened the sense of belonging and trust in leadership and colleagues. Employees gained a better understanding of what was hap-pening across the company and the role they played in our success. Trans-parency, openness, recognition, telling our story—all finally came to light through our efforts.

Having the right tools makes a huge difference in communication effectiveness. In addition to The Barn and email, we are heavily reliant on newer methods of communication such as Slack for instant messaging and focused conversations, and Lattice for public praise and recognition—tied to our Anaplan values. Lattice is a software platform that not only delivers praise to an employee, but you can share it publicly, have it included in the employee's record, and their manager is immediately notified. That's the beauty of Lattice.

Says Linda Lee, Vice President, Executive Communications and Cul-ture at Anaplan, "When we did our first internal communications survey, 97 percent of respondents trusted the information they received from the company. This level of trust is unheard of in most business organizations. You are lucky if you get to 60 percent employee trust in information they receive from their companies, but it was incredible to see we received over 90 percent."

This has been proven over and over again, most recently with our COVID-19 updates starting at the beginning of the pandemic. There was a flood of information and news coverage every day, much of it confusing and conflicting, and we did our best to prioritize the most important and factual information about how travel restrictions, lockdowns, and local regulations were affecting our employees around the globe. We are proud that employ-ees trust the information we send out more than what they see in the news.

We hold a global employee meeting quarterly during which I share key updates and allow time for a Q&A. During the COVID-19 pandemic, we held these sessions weekly at first because things were changing so fast and we needed to communicate frequently through a period of tremendous uncertainty. We have strong engagement overall in these events, in fact, over 90 percent of employees attend all company-wide meetings. This high level of engagement is directly the result of the value our people place on the information we give to them.

We knew that transitioning to 100 percent remote work during that time was a big adjustment, so we had to do more than usual to keep everyone connected and engaged. And it's important for me, as the CEO, to lead these sessions because even as we grow larger and larger, we continue to have this intimate forum where employees can ask me questions directly. I think that's very powerful and it allows me to set the tone and embody the values in a way that is immediate and tangible.

One unexpected benefit of having all of our employee meetings in a virtual format is that our employees feel more connected to me as their CEO. Instead of seeing me from the back of a conference room (or only hearing my voice while my slides were displayed), they now see my face up close on WebEx and feel that I'm talking directly to them. In particular, our employees who were already working remotely before the pandemic appreciated how having everyone attend virtually leveled the playing field—there was no longer an advantage for the people in the room; everyone has equal status in an online meeting. When we held focus groups on envisioning what it would look like to return to physical offices, employees said they didn't want to lose the increased feeling of transparency and intimacy we gained through our frequent online meetings.

When we held our annual user conference, Connected Planning Xperience, in 2020, we completely transformed the event from a two-day, in-person meeting to a curated series of virtual keynotes, panels, and interactive sessions rolled out over a two-week period, and available on-demand thereafter. We were delighted when attendance far exceeded our expectations—we had five times the participation of the normal, in-person event. There was a steep learning curve to master new technology and different techniques for storytelling, but the approach worked so well that we may never go back to doing it the old way.

Slack is an integral communication platform, and it's become even more important while working remotely. Two high-traffic Slack channels we use are #beingfrank, which is my CEO channel where I share quick updates, news, customer success stories, and the occasional selfie; and #AnaplanLOVE, which is focused on our culture and Living Our Values Everyday (LOVE). The #beingfrank channel gives Anaplan employees an inside look into the mind and world of a CEO—it's like my internal Twitter account. On the #AnaplanLOVE channel, every year we hold a competition to see which team can make the best video that explores our values, and we also use the channel to share employee stories and successes. In addition, we also have the AnaplanLOVE Awards, which are given to six individuals who provide a significant business value (directly affecting our results) while living our values. Then, one of the six is chosen as the overall winner who gets to attend the Chairman's Club—our annual top sales performers recognition event.

I firmly believe that CEOs must be active and visible in communicating with employees as much as possible, and should use every opportunity, big or small, to tie back to the company's values and character. It's also critical—no matter what the channel—that communication is two-way, and that I also use these forums as an opportunity to listen. It's essential to listen to be aware of what's most important to employees and on their minds.

Carrying the Culture Flag

Some leaders explicitly consider it their job to create, shape, and influence their company culture—they embrace the role of carrying the culture flag and of modeling upstanding character. And part of their job is to select and surround themselves with people who have strong character. It's in times of adversity when the true character of a company and the people in it are revealed.

Tiger Tyagarajan is President and CEO of Genpact—a professional services firm that specializes in driving digital-led innovation and digitally-enabled intelligent operations for its clients that are mostly Global Fortune 500 companies. Tiger defines a company's culture as how its people behave with one another, and with clients and other stakeholders. When confronted with a situation, what decisions do they make? And how do they behave when no one is watching? According to Tyagarajan, "the long-term, sustainable success of companies is built through culture."

When he and his partners started Genpact, they wanted to build a company where their clients really loved working with them. They wanted the culture of the company to feel the same irrespective of where clients touched it—up and down the organization, anywhere in the world. "At the time," he says, "the culture for us boiled down to 'the only thing that matters is the client.'" He offered the following example to illustrate his point:

> If, in a situation, you are confronted with a choice—on the one hand, direction X, and you think it would be a good direction to take, it will add value to the customer and it will get you your financial goal as well. But then you think the customer is actually asking for Y, and you're scratching your head because you know that is going to hurt

you financially. We are big believers that, in the long term, Y is actually the better decision. Now, you can't do that every time, and you can't do that forever. But we think it's the right thing to do, and it's deep in our culture as a company.[25]

When I asked Tyagarajan how he maintains his unique company culture in an organization that has grown to more than 90,000 people, he explained that he plays a very personal role. He said:

Our clients tell us that one of the reasons they love working with us is because of our culture. One of the ways we maintain it is that the drumbeat never stops. I actually talk about this topic at least once every two or three days—every conversation, every opportunity to talk about culture, I do. And that means that every one of my team has to do the same thing. . . .. I characterize my job as culture building, culture holding, and culture nurturing.[26]

Shantanu Narayen is Chairman, President, and CEO of Adobe, one of world's largest and most diversified software companies. It was Narayen who drove the shift from boxed software to cloud-based subscription software suites, most notably its highly successful Creative Cloud, which contains more than 20 popular desktop and mobile apps including Photoshop, InDesign, Acrobat DC, and more. When he became CEO in 2007, Adobe's market cap was $24 billion.[27] At the time of this writing, it stands at $240 billion.

I asked him to tell me about his perspective on his role—and the role of his team—in modeling character at Adobe. Says Narayen:

I think that in every great corporation, you have different individuals modeling different pieces of character. You have to resonate with it on the culture, but I think there's an acceptance that one individual cannot represent all of the different attributes of character that you want for a successful company. Certainly, character needs to be role modeled by the entire organization, but different individuals play the role of different elements of character that are important. That said, the importance of the leadership team is immense because they are the role models and they set the behaviors in times of adversity. In good times, it's probably not as critical because things naturally go well.[28]

Ultimately, the ideal situation, says Narayen, is when *everyone* in the organization models and lives the culture—reinforcing it through their own day-to-day decisions and actions. The leader sets the tone and hires people who exemplify different aspects of the company's character. And when people don't resonate with a company's character and culture, they need to move on to an organization that is a better fit for them. When everyone is on the same page and working in concert, it paves the way for happy employees, satisfied customers, and breakthrough performance.

Now that we have explored how everyone in an organization can (and should) play a role in creating its core values and culture, in the next chapter, we consider how to make character-led culture your strategy.

CHAPTER 6

Make Character-Led Culture Your Strategy

"Good leadership requires you to surround yourself with people of diverse perspectives who can disagree with you without fear of retaliation."

—*Doris Kearns Goodwin*

It requires a lot of courage to take a stand on behalf of a company's character.

In July 2020, Netflix became the largest entertainment/media company by market cap—less than 25 years after its founding—outpacing long-established industry giants such as Walt Disney Company and Comcast.[1] To say that Netflix's growth "has been rapid" would be perhaps one of the great understatements of the century. And, as you can imagine, all this growth put tremendous strain on the organization and the people who worked in it.

Instrumental to Netflix's success, despite all the obstacles and existential threats it encountered along the way, is a culture that is the foundation of its strategy. This culture-as-strategy determines the decisions its people make, what the company values, performance expectations, promotions and career development, the degree of freedom and responsibility employees enjoy, who gets hired and fired, the investments the company makes, the chances it takes, and much more.

Netflix's unique culture didn't just happen—it is the result of some very intentional choices made by cofounder Reed Hastings and others in the organization, with updates along the way as the company continued to grow and evolve.

In his book *No Rules Rules*, Hastings (with coauthor Erin Meyer) tells the story of how upstart Netflix beat the video entertainment industry heavyweight, Blockbuster, which dominated the industry during the 1990s and early 2000s and then faded into irrelevance and declared bankruptcy in 2010. Says Hastings:

It was not obvious at the time, even to me, but we had one thing that Blockbuster did not: a culture that valued people over process, emphasized innovation over efficiency, and had very few controls. Our culture, which focused on achieving top performance with talent density and leading employees with context not control, has allowed us to continually grow and change as the world, and our members' needs, have likewise morphed around us.[2]

As Netflix points out on its website, "Like all great companies, we strive to hire the best people possible, and we value such things as integrity, excellence, respect, inclusion, and collaboration." However, Netflix also points out five things about its culture that make it stand out from the sea of corporate sameness. What makes Netflix special is how much it:

- Encourages independent decision-making by employees;
- Shares information openly, broadly, and deliberately;
- Is extraordinarily candid with employees;
- Keeps only its highly effective people; and
- Avoids rules.[3]

Hastings explains that when he cofounded Netflix, he wanted to create an organizational culture that would "promote flexibility, employee freedom, and innovation instead of error prevention and rule adherence." At the same time, says Hastings, "I understood that as a company grows, if you don't manage it with policies or control processes, the organization is likely to descend into chaos."[4]

Creating this culture didn't happen overnight. It took time, and much trial and error. However, Hastings and his team kept at it, and eventually they built the kind of culture robust enough to support the company's tremendous growth and ongoing success. Says Hastings:

> If you give employees more freedom instead of developing processes to prevent them from exercising their own judgment, they will make better decisions and it's easier to hold them accountable. This also makes for a happier, more motivated workforce as well as a more nimble company.[5]

For example, when the idea of letting Netflix's employees decide for themselves when and how much vacation they would take was first proposed, it was a radical notion. However, it flowed naturally from the Netflix culture, which encourages independent decision-making by employees—what they call "freedom and responsibility."

One of the key players in the development of the Netflix culture was Patty McCord, who served as Netflix's Chief Talent Officer for 14 years. It was McCord who partnered with Hastings to create the groundbreaking culture manifesto presentation titled, "Netflix Culture: Freedom & Responsibility,"[6] which Facebook COO Sheryl Sandberg said, "may well be the most important document ever to come out of the Valley."[7]

Says McCord about Netflix's vacation non-policy, "You rely on everybody to understand the rhythms of how they work, not just with their manager but with all their coworkers, and make sure everything gets covered."[8]

In other words, you treat them like adults.

To make this work, McCord says that the company put an emphasis on hiring and retaining smart people who could assess situations and make good decisions. She explains, however, that there must be guardrails in place:

> . . .we realized that if we used just the word "freedom," it implied [the freedom] to do anything. We didn't really mean to give people freedom to do anything. We coupled freedom [with] responsibility. It [also] implies reliability and deliverables.[9]

But as McCord readily admits, some Netflix employees couldn't function well in this sort of culture—they weren't able to align themselves with it. As she says, "The freedom and responsibility culture isn't for everybody."[10] And for those who weren't aligned with this or other aspects of the Netflix culture, they either needed to change—which wasn't an easy task for new hires who came from more traditional organizations—or they needed to find another company that was a better fit.

According to Hastings, when you create a culture of freedom and responsibility by removing controls, this triggers a virtuous circle "which attracts top talent and makes possible even fewer controls. All this takes you to a level of speed and innovation that most companies can't match."[11] Again, this cultural transformation doesn't happen overnight. At Netflix, Hastings explains that it took the company three cycles to get its culture to where it is today:

First cycle:

- **Build up talent density** by creating a workforce of high performers.
- **Introduce candor** by encouraging loads of feedback.
- **Remove controls** such as vacation, travel, and expense policies.

Second cycle:

- **Strengthen talent density** by paying top of market.
- **Increase candor** by emphasizing organizational transparency.
- **Release more controls** such as decision-making approvals.

Third cycle:

- **Max up talent density** by implementing the Keeper Test.*
- **Max up candor** by creating circles of feedback.
- **Eliminate most controls** by leading with context not control.

McCord explains that transforming a team or organizational culture is more than just getting in touch with your values. Says McCord:

> The most important thing to understand about transforming a culture, whether that of a team or a whole company, is that it isn't a matter of simply professing a set of values and operating principles. It's a matter of identifying the behaviors that you would like to see become consistent practices and then instilling the discipline of actually doing them.[12]

In other words, amplifying your culture to use it as strategy.

---

*The Netflix Keeper Test is this question: Which of my people, if they told me they were leaving for a similar job at a peer company, would I fight hard to keep at Netflix? (The other people should get a generous severance now so we can open a slot to try to find a star for that role.)

There's a reason why, in career marketplace *Hired*'s most recent survey of tech workers, Netflix was rated the No. 2 public company that respondents said they would most like to work for—just behind Google (No. 1), but ahead of Apple (No. 3), LinkedIn (No. 4), Microsoft (No. 5), Slack (No. 6), and Amazon (No. 7).[13] And there's a reason why Netflix is the world's largest entertainment/media company by market cap—generating more than $20 billion in annual revenue[14] with more than 193 million subscribers all around the world.[15]

I believe it's because Netflix has made character-led culture its strategy.

What's Your Purpose?

When we consider a company's character and core values, there's one more thing we should also consider: its *purpose*. Purpose answers the question, "Why am I here?" And in an organizational context, purpose informs the core values and has a direct impact on culture and employee beliefs, behaviors, and practices.

For some companies, making money and maximizing shareholder value is all that matters. While this is certainly one of the things that business leaders try to do, it's not the only thing, or even the most important thing. Former GE Chairman and CEO Jack Welch once said that focusing just on maximizing shareholder value is "the dumbest idea in the world. Shareholder value is a result, not a strategy. Your main constituencies are your employees, your customers, and your products."[16]

Fortunately, many CEOs agree with Welch's assessment. The Business Roundtable is an association of CEOs of America's leading companies—collectively employing more than 15 million people with more than $7 trillion in annual revenues. The group "promotes a thriving U.S. economy and expanded opportunities for all Americans through sound public policies."[17] In 2019, Business Roundtable released a new Statement on the Purpose of a Corporation. The document was signed by 181 CEOs who committed to focus on more than just making money for shareholders; they pledged to lead their companies for the benefit of *all* stakeholders, including customers, employees, suppliers, communities, and shareholders.

The following five commitments are at the heart of Business Roundtable's Statement on the Purpose of a Corporation:

- **Delivering value to our customers.** We will further the tradition of American companies leading the way in meeting or exceeding customer expectations.

- **Investing in our employees.** This starts with compensating them fairly and providing important benefits. It also includes supporting them through training and education that help develop new skills for a rapidly changing world. We foster diversity and inclusion, dignity and respect.
- **Dealing fairly and ethically with our suppliers.** We are dedicated to serving as good partners to the other companies, large and small, that help us meet our missions.
- **Supporting the communities in which we work.** We respect the people in our communities and protect the environment by embracing sustainable practices across our businesses.
- **Generating long-term value for shareholders, who provide the capital that allows companies to invest, grow, and innovate.** We are committed to transparency and effective engagement with shareholders.[18]

This group of CEOs does not believe that its responsibility begins and ends with making money—there's much more to it than that. The CEOS know that when organizations serve *all* of their stakeholders—including employees, customers, vendors, and the community—they create a sense of purpose that unlocks the engagement and motivation of their people. Creating shareholder wealth is certainly important—you need investors to provide the cash necessary to fund your growth. But true purpose goes deeper than that.

Deloitte surveyed more than 1,000 full-time workers at a variety of organizations that employed at least 100 people—finding that 82 percent of people working for an organization with a strong sense of purpose said they were confident that their organization would grow this year. When it came to organizations *without* a strong sense of purpose, however, only 48 percent of employees reported that they were confident that their organization would grow this year.[19]

In addition, as part of Deloitte Global's 2020 Global Millennial Survey, more than 27,000 Millennials and Gen Z workers were surveyed to gain an understanding of how much they value businesses mirroring their commitment to society, putting people ahead of profits, and prioritizing environmental sustainability. Respondents who feel their employers are creating diverse and inclusive work environments rose to 71 percent, "Having a positive impact on communities" improved to 69 percent, and 61 percent said that "Reducing its impact on the environment" is one of the things they value.[20]

Purpose *matters*.

I asked Kirsten Rhodes, San Francisco Managing Principal at Deloitte, to tell me more about the firm's purpose. Says Rhodes:

> Purpose is consistently and constantly talked about at Deloitte—as our commitment to purpose is core to who we are. Purpose serves as a compass that guides our culture, our decision-making, and our vision for Deloitte's future. The work we do has allowed us to make an impact that matters for our people, our clients, and our communities.
>
> We live in a time where we urgently need unity and purpose. This has been further underscored by the COVID-19 pandemic and systemic racial injustices that continue to plague our society. The complexity of these and other societal issues requires us to navigate them as a collective business community. No single enterprise has all of the solutions, which is why we're teaming with others in the business ecosystem to create meaningful and lasting change, to advance an economy that delivers inclusive prosperity.[21]

As leaders, we are in the unique position to mobilize and align our people around a collective purpose, and to make our organizations more *purposeful*—attracting the best people, customers, investors, and others to join with us in our quest to change the world for the better. To accomplish this, it's up to us to create an inspiring vision of the future that can be translated into strategy and execution.

During the time I was Cisco's CFO, we reached a crossroads in our growth. We were a large company—66,000+ people—and very successful for a number of years in the switching and routing markets. But our future growth would require moving into some diversified new markets outside of switching and routing, while keeping everybody aligned and also driving success.

So, how did we do it?

We knew we would need to create a vision for where we wanted to go, and we would have to create a strategy to get there. But the key to our success would require getting that vision clearly identified at a company level, aligning it to a strategy, and then making sure there were initiatives that would help support that strategy—all while making sure that our employees knew about our new vision and embraced it.

The biggest challenge in any organization, but especially large organizations, is when people don't have a clear sense of how they contribute to the big picture. When you understand what the company's highest purpose is and how your day-to-day work supports it, the value of your work to achieve the collaborative purpose is clear. Aligning purpose and contributed value is when our work is most engaging. Organizations delivering on their purpose mobilize people—and build loyalty—by virtue of that alignment.

In business as in sports, it's important to operate as a team. When you have a coach who is there and able to tell everyone, "Here are the plays," you're much more likely to win the game when everyone has the same expectations and objectives than if everybody gets on the field and just decides what to do on their own, with no coordinated strategy. It's the same in business. If every department does what it wants to do, with no overall vision keeping them aligned to their purpose, then execution is certain to suffer with all sorts of negative outcomes. As explained in a Cisco white paper published while I was at the company:

> When departments work toward their own isolated goals, they tend to protect their information and assets instead of sharing them, and they often compete with other departments for opportunities and resources. Knowledge that others in the organization could benefit from gets trapped in silos. Overlaps develop. Budget monies are wasted. All the while, markets move and new opportunities emerge.[22]

To ensure that everyone was aligned and working effectively toward Cisco's most important priorities, CEO John Chambers developed a common vocabulary for making decisions. This common vocabulary consisted of four terms: vision, strategy, execution, and metrics, which we usually just referred to as "VSEM" for short.

- **Vision.** Communicates a team's shared view of success.
- **Strategy.** Represents important decisions for where and how to apply resources to accomplish the vision.
- **Execution.** Outlines critical initiatives, programs, or actions that support each strategy.
- **Metrics.** Shows how the team measures success and agrees to be held accountable to the execution plan.

VSEM is a way of saying, "Okay—here's the playbook: what we do, how we do it, why we do it, and your part in it." At Cisco, it would start at the highest level then cascade down to the next level, so that everyone would know where they fit in the overall playbook. As a result, everyone in the organization—from the executive team on down to frontline employees—was in alignment. We were all pulling together instead of having each department do its own thing.

I brought VSEM with me to Anaplan, and I think it had a tremendously positive impact on our culture because people got to understand and appreciate what success looks like—this is what we're trying to accomplish and how. It also gave people a way to answer key questions like, "Is this really something I should be doing today—is this helping me get to that?" People may be working at their limits, but it's meaningful because they can clearly see where the organization is going, and how they contribute to achieving the company's vision. Our priorities are aligned and we're accountable to a shared target.

And, ultimately, an organization's purpose drives the vision, which leads to the strategies we decide to pursue and the way we execute on them. Purpose also drives culture, which, in turn, drives individual and company performance. When employees believe in the company's purpose, they are energized and motivated to do their best work. When purpose is communicated openly and with intention, people understand what's expected of them and that their contributions matter. Having a shared purpose enhances collaboration among teams, so they work together to get results. Every organization I've worked for that had a great culture driven by a sense of collective purpose has benefited from its resulting resilience.

Anaplan's vision statement—*turn change into advantage*—serves to define the capability we deliver for our customers. It acknowledges the business reality that constant change, disruption, and complexity put pressure on teams to perpetually adapt to new information, opportunities, and crises. We've all heard the adage: *The only constant is change.* The Anaplan platform gives customers the capability to systematically adapt to change, building agility and resilience into the DNA of their business so that an always-on ability to change becomes a competitive advantage.

We fundamentally believe connecting people with data, insights, and plans across the enterprise drives the best business decisions that yield the best possible performance. What we're really doing is empowering people to collaborate with one another—to apply their unique acumen and creativity to contribute to their company's collective best work. And that is where we zero in on **our purpose**: *empowering people to contribute their best selves.* That is our reason for being. Anaplan's value proposition as an employer is based on the same foundation of inclusivity: to provide a workplace where each person feels seen, heard, and valued, and can contribute their unique talent to our collective effort because we fundamentally believe every colleague brings unique value that enriches our whole. We believe that for ourselves and for our customers.

Our purpose contributes to our hypergrowth. We're creating transformative business value as we help customers orchestrate better performance across finance, workforces, supply chains, sales, and marketing. That value resonates on a personal level too. I hear time and again from people using our platform about the difference it makes to their professional lives and their careers—it's emotional for them. They are contributing to their organizations more effectively and that's professionally fulfilling. They're spending more time with their families. They're getting recognized for their performance and promoted. And they're enjoying work more.

Within Anaplan, our intention is to create the context in which people can do their best work. That intention extends to our partner ecosystem, which we've significantly grown over the last few years. And perhaps it's no surprise that our purpose has changed the lives of our customers, both professionally and personally.

I was recently talking with a new customer's head of sales operations, and he explained that the selection process we had just gone through was very competitive—they interviewed many vendors. He told me that Anaplan stood out among the other vendors because of the personal interactions the selection team had with our people, and how we connected with them. According to this head of sales operations, all the other vendors were very tactically focused on the technical aspects and capabilities of their product offerings, but they didn't make the people connection the way we did.

I think you can really gain an understanding of the character of a company when things go wrong. Sara Baxter Orr told me about an experience with Anaplan when she was still working for Verizon. We were working with the company to create a top-line, enterprise revenue planning and territory management system, which was an incredibly complex effort. When we flipped the switch, the system crashed. Anaplan worked closely with the Verizon team to troubleshoot, get back on track, and turn failure into success, which we ultimately did, creating a stronger and deeper relationship with our client that continues to this day.

According to Baxter Orr, the interaction our people had with her team was different than she had experienced with other vendors. "It felt like there was a personal commitment from the Anaplan team," says Baxter Orr. "I knew that you wanted us to succeed. There's always a human element to anything in business, and we really felt it from the people we worked with in Anaplan. It was comforting."

These words were echoed by Claire Lord, who regularly interacted with Anaplan people when she was at Thomas Cook. As Lord told me, "I've heard lots of companies say, "It's customer first," and you take it with a grain of salt. But, when I was Anaplan's customer, it felt like that was the truth. And being a part of Anaplan now, it's been fantastic for me to see that really is the case. The customer does come first, which is really refreshing to say."

Responses such as these from our customers (and former customers, now Anaplan employees) are a direct reflection of our purpose and embody our character. It's something we live and breathe, and our customers respond to it, just as our people and other stakeholders do.

I know for certain that being *of this era* is good business. The business environment has evolved tremendously from the time I was at IBM decades ago to the current day here at Anaplan, and this evolution has a direct impact on our purpose as a business. We're engaging more with community issues, whether it's systemic racism, affordable housing, homelessness, or the environment, and our people are more attuned to what's going on in the world around us. They want to make a positive difference in the world, and so do I—both personally and as CEO of this company. It's why I serve as a member of the Bay Area Council, a 70-year-old civic, business, and political partnership focused on strong economic health of the region, balancing long-term economic, social, and environmental sustainability.

All of this goes to the reason why we're here. Clarity of purpose guides how we spend our time and attention—whether creating products and service for our customers, a great place to work for our employees, or vibrant and strong communities where we live and work. It's all part of upstanding company character.

Beyond Financial Results

Anaplan solves really complex problems in a unique and differentiated way. Our value proposition to customers is, ultimately, greater operational and financial success. We run our own business by targeting the financial results that will optimize shareholder return over time. But that's just one way we run our business. Our success is not defined just by financial results. As I mentioned earlier in this chapter, narrowly focusing on financial outcomes is not enough. Ultimately, maintaining a good company culture and attracting and retaining the very best people require paying attention to more than the bottom line. We must actively manage to company character in order to also deliver on our company purpose.

In Chapter 1, I mentioned the nickname Anaplan had earned by the time I arrived as CEO in 2017: "Manaplan." This reflected our male-dominated executive and management team. Women and people of color literally did not sit at the table—in the large conference room they sat in chairs along the wall, seen but rarely heard in between all the mansplaining.

Simon Tucker, our Chief Planning Officer, was around in those days, in fact, he was one of the earliest employees. In an interview, he described what this culture was like:

> Four years ago, the Anaplan culture was chaotic—it was like an old boys' club that didn't include certain people, particularly women. It was a toxic, aggressive workplace, and that permeated throughout the organization. It was not how you should behave or treat employees. Our culture has evolved tremendously since then.[23]

I had gained a great appreciation for diversity during my time in college in New York City, where I was exposed to a wide variety of people and perspectives and experiences. And that just grew as I traveled the world during my professional career. So, when I walked into Anaplan in 2017 and I saw this noticeable gender exclusion and lack of diversity in general, it was a shock to me—it was completely unexpected. And I knew that this culture wasn't just wrong, but that it would be a major obstacle to our success.

The company did have some other challenges when I arrived. Anaplan had been without a leader for over a year, and the board was contemplating what to do with the company. It had a lot of potential, but was not on track to realize it. We had other things that needed to be changed as a part of our culture, but our lack of diversity and inclusion was the most glaring. The culture was such that women were sidelined and drowned out. I remember thinking to myself, "Are we back in the '50s?"

So, we set out to redefine the culture. I hired Linda Lee to lead Culture and Communications, then Marilyn Miller to serve as our Chief People Officer. We brought in YY Lee, who serves as our Chief Strategy Officer, and Ana Pinczuk, who is our Chief Development Officer, which encompasses Engineering and Product. I recruited Sue Bostrom and Yvonne Wassenaar to join the board of directors. Today, strong, experienced women not only occupy a growing share of seats at the Anaplan leadership table, but their voices and ideas shape our business. While I'm proud of our progress, I know that building an equitable, inclusive workplace will always be a work in progress, a never-ending quest.

As I was working on this book, I pulled together a group of longtime Anaplan employees to ask them about the changes they personally experienced as we transitioned to today's Anaplan. Says Melissa Schwartz, Director of Sales, Strategic Accounts:

> When I first started with the company eight years ago, there were very few women. It was very male-oriented. There was a turning point, however, when they started to look at who was really performing. And that's when they started to recognize that a lot of high performers here were actually working moms.
>
> So, that was the start of an appreciation. Yeah, we're working moms. We're balancing family and work. But we can do it and we can do a good job at it. But, quite frankly, we had to break through what may have been a more traditional bias around being a working mom. I think today it's almost a marker of pride that we are able to not only do well and balance all of it, but it is welcomed here and supported.[24]

Deb Kennedy, Majors Regional Vice President, pointed out that the culture definitely shifted after I began hiring women onto the executive leadership team. Explains Kennedy:

> When you and Marilyn arrived, it changed the game for those of us who wanted to move up. I've been in sales for a long time and people tend to hire their buddies. And if all the buddies are male, then that's who's going to get hired. Sales is very much a relationship-driven function.
>
> So, it's a mindset change—it has to start somewhere. It was suddenly like, wait a minute, let's see if there's anyone internally qualified who we can give a shot at moving up. I appreciated that, and I think it was a huge change in our sales mentality. But it requires senior leadership constantly asking, "Why aren't these women being considered?"[25]

Allison Grieb, Regional Vice President, Bay Area Sales, echoed Kennedy's comments about the change in culture over the past few years, particularly for women. Says Grieb:

> You brought a level of integrity and awareness that, frankly, we didn't have before. I think the women who succeeded before were going to

succeed no matter what the circumstance. But now we have an opportunity not just to level set, but to help women drive toward and become leaders in the organization.[26]

Organizations make their company character apparent in a variety of ways, but perhaps no more so than in how they support every employee and provide him or her with opportunities to excel. When they do, their people will become fully engaged and loyal long-term additions to the team, consistently delivering positive business outcomes. Ana Pinczuk described to me how her previous employers set the bar high for what she expected at Anaplan:

> There was a sense of loyalty at AT&T, and the same was true at Cisco. I worked at AT&T for 15 years because I was so aligned with the character of the company. It was a company that early on supported equal opportunity and supported women—and this was super important to me. They also invested in your career, they did what was right for the environment, and I think these things matter even more to people today. They have to be much more immediate, and if they're not there, people walk.[27]

As CEO, I'm responsible for a lot more than the bottom line. I also have to keep an eye on our culture because our culture affects our financial results and our overall health as a company. I asked Doug Merritt, President and CEO of Splunk, how he balances the financial and nonfinancial aspects of managing his company. Says Merritt:

> A company I worked for before Splunk had more of a scarcity mindset, which is diametrically opposed to an abundance mindset. People describe me as very optimistic about the future—big-picture oriented, and maybe not as focused on detailed numbers every single day.
>
> When I arrived at Splunk, which at the time claimed a greater than $50 billion total addressable market, I was surprised to see a degree of scarcity thinking that I didn't expect with a growth company. I actually do care a lot about numbers, but, if you are a $300 million revenue company in a $50 billion+ TAM, logic and abundance thinking would tell you that the focus should be on capturing as much of that TAM as quickly as possible. Instead, we were grinding every contract to the last dollar and defending every term and condition.

The dissonance was confusing to me. If we're preaching massive opportunity, then the company has to be geared to capture that opportunity. Abundance is so pervasive, we've got to move quickly, we've got to be willing to go after this huge market opportunity.

In a situation like this, I would rather be directionally right and execute rapidly than be precise and execute carefully. That thinking is generally true in my life, but it's absolutely true with Splunk given how big the opportunity is. Let's find a way to generate and sustain momentum to ensure the flywheel is turning faster and faster.[28]

Merritt has built a strong, customer-centered culture at Splunk. In fact, customer success is the company's number one priority above all else. According to Merritt:

> Our top three company priorities, in order, are customer success, world-class products and services, and top talent. Why did we come out with three priorities, in that order of importance? To help empower our employees in their decision making. For example, where I've seen this work really well is when a customer is in trouble. Does it make sense to fly five people in and spend half a million dollars to make a company whole? On a P&L basis, I'm sure it doesn't. But if customer success is your No. 1 mantra, it does. I wanted to create a framework for people that was really clear. At Splunk, we believe as a group that without a healthy customer, we have no business. Of course, to support our customers, we have to have a world-class, high-quality set of products and services, and that's not going to happen without amazing employees who are bought into our culture and who are learning and growing. But our customers and their success are at the center of all we do.[29]

Learnings from the Disney Institute

Walt Disney Parks, Experiences, and Products—which includes everything from amusement parks such as Disneyland and Walt Disney World to the Disney Cruise Line and National Geographic Expeditions to consumer products such as toys, food, and more—is well known for its extensive employee training programs. The organization's frontline employees, known within the Disney parks and resorts as "Cast Members," are key to the continued success of this important member of the Disney family. In fact, Walt Disney

Parks, Experiences, and Products contributed almost 40 percent of the Walt Disney Company's overall revenues of $69.6 billion in 2019—the largest amount of any of Disney's four major business segments.[30]

Because of this success in training its Cast Members, for years, the Walt Disney Company was approached by executives of other companies, all asking the same question: "How do you do it?" After answering this question who knows how many times, Disney realized that they could build a business around their proprietary employee-training programs and techniques. Thus was born the Disney Institute, which today offers a variety of professional development courses in leadership, employee engagement, and service; customer experience summits and data and analytics conferences; advisory services; and keynote speakers and behind-the-scenes tours for corporate meetings and conventions.

In May 2017, we sent a group of Anaplan leaders to the Disney Institute in California with the intention of seeing how we could bring some of the Disney magic into our company. The Anaplan team attended courses in leadership excellence, employee engagement, and quality service, and learned key lessons along the way. One of the most important of these lessons was summarized as follows:

> Disney's consistent business results are driven by **over-managing** certain things that most companies undermanage or ignore—and that is a key source of what differentiates us. We have learned to be **intentional** where others are unintentional.

This statement is an example of something that is very distinctive and defining about Disney's culture—the fact that they "care too much" about details that others would overlook. They do this because they are so singularly focused on making guest experiences great. During the course of the Disney Institute experience, our team heard all sorts of stories that illustrated what "caring too much" looks like in practice, for example:

- Walt Disney was concerned that after a long, exhausting day at Disneyland, families wouldn't be able to find their cars in the sprawling parking lots surrounding the park. So, he came up with two systems to solve this problem. The first system was to create signs with pictures of Disney characters, numbers, and colors—all to help guests remember how to get to their cars at the end of the day. Women remember pictures; men remember numbers, and kids remember colors. The second system was to ask a lost family, "What time did you arrive?" If the response was, "9:15 a.m." the parking attendant would know exactly where you parked because they arrange cars in areas by time slot, and the attendant could lead you right to that area. This is why there's never a lost family in Disney's parking lots.

- Walt Disney also sourced covered trashcans for the theme park, a design that was rare at the time. He had them positioned every six feet and made sure they were beautiful and blended into the design of the park. This strategy ensured that litter and overflowing trash never marred Disneyland's squeaky-clean atmosphere.

- When Disney got into the cruise business, it quickly discovered that its cruise ship's 150 inside staterooms without windows caused motion sickness for some passengers. So, the design/production team created inside staterooms with faux windows called Magical Portholes to reduce motion sickness. The Magical Portholes use four high-definition cameras on the exterior of the ship to feed live video to wall-mounted monitors on the wall in the round shape of a porthole. The four video feeds correspond to the location of each stateroom—forward, aft, starboard, or port. To increase the magic even more, the designers created three dozen animated characters—including Dumbo the flying elephant and Mickey Mouse—that would randomly pass by the Magical Portholes during the course of each day.[31]

Disney builds a deep sense of pride with the values it instills in its new recruits from day one. Every new employee goes through an intensive, three-to-five-day training process at a specialized facility custom built for the task. The first day on the job, every new Disney Cast Member attends the Disney Traditions training, where each learns Disney language and symbols, heritage and traditions, quality standards, values, and traits and behaviors.

As you would expect, Disney has a very careful hiring process to ensure the people it brings on-board are going to embody the culture and values through and through. One time the company was recruiting to fill a position on the executive team. It had found a top-notch candidate who it thought would be a perfect addition. His qualifications were impressive, and he made it to the final round of interviews where the company evaluates culture fit. The final interviewer mentioned to the candidate how excited he was at the prospect of parking strollers with him on Christmas, one of the busiest days of the year for the park. The candidate scoffed at the idea. Even though he was a perfect match for the role in every other way, he wasn't hired because he felt that parking strollers was beneath him. This attitude was not a fit with Disney's culture.

At Anaplan, we do our best to be thoughtful and intentional, and to ensure that we recruit and retain people who are fully aligned with our values and culture. We may not always get it right, but we strive to find people of upstanding character who want to grow with us while creating value for our customers.

Transparency and Accountability

There are two more things I would like to cover in this chapter about making character-led culture your strategy: transparency and accountability. As we address issues such as diversity and inclusion, it's critical that we have constructive dialogues with our people. These constructive dialogues depend on absolute transparency and candor on the part of everyone involved.

At Anaplan, we have established a strong culture and set of core values. We thrive on diversity and inclusion, and we have designed a hiring process and working environment in which *all* people are respected and valued. It's important to me personally, just as it should be to every one of us who works for this company, that we honor our culture and live our core values. As a company, we are very clear on what our values are—we are as transparent about them as we can possibly be. We publish them, provide training on them, rate performance against them, and hire and fire based on them. They are the North Star that guides our decision-making. They are the guardrails that guide our behavior.

Ultimately, I believe that being transparent in our beliefs attracts the very best people to our company, and once they are here, I believe it encourages them to stay. We want everyone to have a voice in how we do business, and in the contributions they can make to serve our customers by solving their difficult problems. We also know that not everyone—in and out of the company—is going to agree 100 percent with every internal decision or policy. That's okay. We are open to feedback and constructive dialogue, and part of being authentic and acting like an owner is being able to speak up and voice opinions and ideas. But that doesn't mean anything goes; if someone is fundamentally at odds with elements of our culture or values, then we may have to part ways. We have to draw the line.

It requires a lot of courage on the part of an executive team to take a stand on behalf of a company's character and to create those boundaries and to say, "You may not agree, you may not feel good about this, but this is our fundamental character. We're listening, but these are the lanes we're in."

The wave of protests against racism and injustice that washed across the country in 2020 put most modern companies into completely uncharted territory. Many companies have a set of core values—traits like integrity and trust and innovation—but what's different now is there's an entirely new level of personal accountability. It's not enough for leaders to just stand behind the persona of the company, behind the core values—there's a much greater expectation now for executives to have upstanding personal character.

In our own meetings with employees, and in our internal communication platforms such as Slack, we're being asked difficult, often complex, questions about where the company stands. In some cases, we're being lauded for what we've accomplished, and in others, we're being taken to task for what we have yet to achieve. I think it's important that every employee feels safe to express his or her feelings honestly and transparently, without fear of repercussion. Says Marilyn Miller, our Chief People Officer:

> We don't allow anonymity in our internal company meetings. If you want to ask Frank a question, you are more than entitled to do that. We ask that you do it respectfully and that you identify yourself for accountability. What I love about that is it hasn't stopped him from being asked very difficult and complicated questions, which is the point.[32]

According to Miller, the overall trend is toward more transparency and less anonymity. A healthy corporate culture has high levels of trust, and for trust to exist, you have to know who you're dealing with. She says:

> When people first started communicating online, anonymity gave a certain protection and then a certain value. Now, for the first time, you're seeing more people stepping out of the shadows. Slack's not anonymous. LinkedIn's not anonymous. You're seeing a lot more voices being shared in non-anonymous ways. Transparency and accountability are evolving.[33]

More and more, there's an expectation of accountability for the positions we take and the decisions we make coming from both inside and outside the organization—via internal surveys, social media, LinkedIn, Twitter, Glassdoor, and more. Ultimately, transparency and accountability create pressure for individuals and organizations to do the right thing—which is what upstanding character is all about.

A company's character attracts us as consumers and as employees, and it's one of the most important qualities that keeps us there. I think about the aura that, for example, Apple has created around its products and organization—the combination of cutting-edge technology, beautiful design, and great marketing. The Apple culture attracts buyers to its products and it attracts people who want to work at an innovative company that is pushing the boundaries of what's possible. As the company says to prospective recruits on its website, "Join us. Be you."[34]

Making character-led culture your strategy is just good business. When you intentionally nurture culture—walking your values' talk—you can build followership. The stakeholder relationships with employees, customers, partners, and all their communities must be mutually beneficial. Your ability as leaders to balance the two-way stakes defines long-term success and builds a new dimension to competitive advantage. We've long counted brand goodwill as part of company valuations. Your call to action is to actively engage and nurture upstanding company character as much as you would any other company asset.

CHAPTER 7

Magnetic Character: Activating Positive Forces

"If you stand for nothing, Burr, what will you fall for?"
—*Lin-Manuel Miranda as Alexander Hamilton in the musical* Hamilton

Take bold action to drive positive change.

This might be the most important chapter of this book. If you do nothing else, your call to action is to identify the environmental, social, or governance (ESG) issues that will test your company character. How you face them will affect your immediate and long-term reputation. You must decide whether those positions will be active or passive—making those decisions with intention and activating plans where needed. Ignore the call at your own peril. The risk is letting negative forces of offline character offend people you need for success instead of activating positive forces of upstanding character to attract loyal followers.

I recently joined a group of CEOs convened by Google. The discussion topic was the change in sensibility toward business leaders engaging on ESG issues directly and indirectly affecting their companies. The consensus: Engaging is no longer optional. Now is the moment for businesses and brands to figure out what they will stand for—which happens to also be a tenet of upstanding character. Figuring out what you think about and will do on matters of social justice, inclusion, climate change, or pay equity, for example, can energize the magnetic, positive forces of company character, helping your organization attract and retain loyal employee, customer, and investor followings that strengthen companies.

Taking a Stand

It's clear to me that our societal expectations are totally different today than they were five years, or even just a year ago. Today, we are experiencing significant social change, and leaders are being challenged like never before. Most people want the companies they work for to actively support and advocate for a variety of national and global issues, including diversity and inclusion, civil rights, racial justice, renewable energy, and climate change, with more being added to the list. And, as we know from our own experience as consumers, most people want to buy from companies that support the same issues they do.

Historically, executive leadership teams have been tasked with driving performance, getting results, execution, personal accountability, and delivering for shareholders. As I've noted earlier, the new leadership mandate goes beyond solely managing operational and financial results. Our expanded purpose is to serve all stakeholders. While corporate social responsibility matured over the last two decades and corporate philanthropy has become common for companies of all sizes, we're entering an evolution of the role of business in society.

In the era we're leaving behind, part of being *professional* as a leader meant not discussing personal opinions on topics not related to the business. In the office, I remember when it was considered bad form to talk about polarizing societal issues, and you especially didn't discuss those topics in your official leadership capacity. Those times are now gone.

Today, we must embrace our shared stake in issues that have the potential to marginalize or imperil the lives of our colleagues and communities. It does not matter how directly or indirectly they are related to our core business. What matters is acting on the recognition that business must serve a larger purpose than its immediate self-interest. Trust in governments and news media has eroded dramatically around the world. Amplified and aggregated voices on social media can make or break business reputations within moments or months. Whether as employees or consumers, people are looking to the business sector for leadership and are monitoring leaders and companies to see how they demonstrate character. What you say and what you do—or don't do—plays on a larger stage and will attract or turn off people more than ever before.

All to say, it is now imperative to develop thoughtful and holistic points of view and strategies on social and environmental issues. Leaders now must take stands for not only their work domains, but for society too. That starts with personal convictions and declaring and acting upon those convictions as a leader and as a business. The online character framework presented in Chapter 3 can help you chart your course.

From my personal experience going through this right now, companies and their leaders can't be silent on racial justice or sustainability as an example. When we are silent on issues that matter, people will fill in the gaps themselves—and most likely negatively. If we don't convey and demonstrate our support for diversity and inclusion, then top candidates will pass us by—looking for employers that do. If we don't talk about our stance on climate change, they'll assume we don't *care* about climate change, when we actually do.

Navigating this increased expectation to weigh in on societal issues can be fraught for companies. As Marilyn Miller articulated in Chapter 3 about the DNA of upstanding character, we have to be deliberate when we take positions—or make the decision not to. Taking stands on social issues always risks making one group of stakeholders happy while alienating others. But today, not taking any position is just as fraught.

Consider the example of David Barrett, CEO of San Francisco–based Expensify. Barrett sent an email to 10 million users of the company's software product in support of then-presidential candidate Joe Biden. In part, the email read, "Anything less than a vote for Biden is a vote against democracy."[1] Given that nearly half of the electorate voted for Biden's opponent, it's probable that many of his customers disagreed with this sentiment.

In contrast, Brian Armstrong, CEO of cryptocurrency platform Coinbase, announced in a blog post that the company would no longer comment on causes not directly related to the company's mission, including broader societal issues. In his words, "We don't advocate for any particular causes or candidates internally that are unrelated to our mission because it is a distraction from our mission. Even if we all agree something is a problem, we may not all agree on the solution."[2] At the moment when business declarations of support for racial justice were expected, Armstrong was saying his organization would not take a position.

According to news reports, Coinbase employees were offered a severance payment of four to six months' pay if they decided they wanted to leave the company after this announcement. Sixty employees (about 5 percent of the workforce) voted with their feet and took Coinbase up on its offer.[3] However, as many have pointed out, choosing not to engage is still a choice—one that can be seen as aligning the company with an unjust status quo.

These opposing examples—acting on a polarizing conviction or disengaging from any point of view—demonstrate the need for a whole new way to frame for ourselves and for our businesses what and how we will lead beyond our missions.

A Continuum for Change

I believe all leaders today need to give serious thought to the role they and their organizations can and should play in addressing the social, societal, and economic macro issues of our time. Key to this thought process is determining your own personal comfort levels in addressing these issues—the work Cy Wakeman suggests in Chapter 3 to develop the clarity needed to lead with character. But there's a strategic evaluation to make just as critically. Not every issue will make sense for your business to act on. Having declared positions that reflect your purpose and values can itself be worthwhile. As with every other facet of business performance, focus drives results.

My team and I are using a three-part working framework to help us segment our approach to macro issues: a continuum from position to agenda to activism.

Position: When we take a position, we're clarifying and speaking out publicly on an issue and taking a stand. For example, Anaplan joined the chorus of business support for the Black Lives Matter movement when I posted this message of solidarity to LinkedIn in the days after George Floyd was murdered: "Black Lives Matter. We stand with the Black Community. We adamantly believe diversity makes us stronger. We cannot allow further racial and social injustice. We must do better through justice, empathy, and compassion. We will work with community leaders, philanthropy groups, and donate to help stop systemic racism. Justice for George Floyd. Ahmaud Arbery. Breonna Taylor."[4]

You can decide what issues you want to focus on and what positions you and your organization want to take—in support or against them. But you must be prepared to be held accountable for living up to the stated position. You will be called out internally and externally if your policies and execution don't line up with your words. When your reputation is at stake, you need to make thoughtful and holistic decisions on which issues to speak out about.

Agenda: Creating an agenda goes beyond simply taking a position. It's making a plan of action that puts your people and organization in motion in support of some social, societal, or economic macro issue. This could involve setting goals for workforce diversity, creating systems for recruiting a more diverse workforce, ensuring that everyone feels a sense of belonging and that they have a meaningful voice in the organization, and then measuring progress.

At Anaplan, the executive leadership team felt strongly that advancing our agenda for an equitable and inclusive workplace must include increased understanding of and addressing our own personal and professional biases. My direct reports and I embarked on an intense diversity, equity, and inclusion training program to examine our current cultural practices, help refine policies and practices that further support equity and inclusion, and invest in personal and professional development. We have engaged Leverage-2Lead to work with us as a team and individually to educate, inform, coach, and re-examine the degree to which we live our values and accelerate our own personal growth.[5]

For me, this has not only been an eye-opening experience, but it has allowed our executive leadership team to be vulnerable and open with one another like never before. Our deeply moving and revealing work with Leverage2Lead is ongoing as of this writing, and my direct reports and I are actively engaged, influenced, educated, informed, and trained, and we are doing the hard and painstaking work of examining our own biases and shifting our mindsets. I strongly believe this work will have a lasting impact on our entire ecosystem for the better.

Activism: In some cases, it may be right for your business to take a much more active external role in advocating and driving change on specific macro issues. When you move along the continuum to activism, you might decide to contribute money or expertise to a cause (e.g., Coca-Cola, Nike, and Apple have made contributions to advocacy organizations for criminal justice reform),[6] support legislation or policy that will help solve an issue, or mobilize people to a cause by organizing or fundraising or convening for action. You'll read in the following about two initiatives we proudly back to catalyze economic opportunity for underrepresented people and provide a means to drive systemic change in workplace experiences.

Using the position/agenda/activism framework can help you segment and focus your attention. My leadership team and I have used the framework to prioritize issues where we are in a particularly good position to move the needle, while being transparent about others where we are not. For example, our organization has a relatively small carbon footprint, so the issue of climate change for us falls between position and agenda. Our position is that business should conduct itself in environmentally responsible ways, and our agenda is to minimize our environmental impact by adhering to workplace best practices (e.g., energy-efficient facilities and recycling programs).

On racial justice issues, our positions are clear. We emphatically believe Black lives matter. We also believe access to economic opportunity must be improved for underrepresented communities. And as an employer, we can make a difference. Our agenda is to increase the number and improve the experiences of people of color in the technology sector. Our activism extends to how we're doing both of those things to benefit not only Anaplan, but our partners, customers, and industry colleagues as well. The following are two examples of how we are doing just that.

Investing in career opportunities for underrepresented people

Data literacy is becoming the most important skill for the future of work. To create career opportunity for diverse talent, we are partnering with Correlation One, a technology company whose mission is to create a diverse talent pool for data science, to sponsor their DS4A ("Data Science For All") Empowerment initiative.

The DS4A ambition is bold: to train 10,000 talented Black, Hispanic, and other individuals from underrepresented minorities by 2022 in data and analytics for free, and connect each one with a mentor, to create equal access to the jobs of tomorrow. We believe, as Correlation One does, that it will take novel talent strategies for companies to effectively compete in their industries and increase diversity in technical fields.

This targeted program will recruit, train, and provide career connections to underrepresented groups to help them fast-track future-ready careers. Every one of Anaplan's customers and partners is working on digital transformations, for which artificial intelligence and data science expertise is essential. So, this work is close to home for Anaplan, and we believe its community-building and mentoring approach will accelerate lucrative job opportunities for people of color.

We invited the co-CEOs of Correlation One, Sham Mustafa and Rasheed Sabar, to Anaplan to talk about what inspired them to start their DS4A Empowerment initiative. Says Mustafa:

> Data science and artificial intelligence are going to be the most transformative technologies of our time. The data revolution is coming really fast and hundreds of millions of people need to be upskilled—they need to be data literate and they need access to learn these skills to participate in the data economy.

Adds Sabar:

These are the jobs of the future, but success is not equally distributed. We've all heard the horror stories of algorithmic bias, for example facial recognition software not recognizing the faces of Black people. Now is the time to decide how we want to build a global data ecosystem and make it inclusive. You hear CEOs saying, "I can't find enough qualified underrepresented people to hire." There's a shortage in the supply of diverse talent, so our idea is let's go and create that supply of underrepresented talent by offering completely free technical training along with mentorship, social capital, and ultimately a pathway to jobs. We launched in October 2020 and our first cohort of Fellows is 60 percent Black, 30 percent Hispanic, 15 percent LGBTQ, and more than half women.

Our early progress with the program Mustafa and Sabar have designed has been transformative for us and program participants. We're already planning for the second cohort of DS4A Fellows. I'm proud of the work we're doing with Correlation One and commend it for making an incredible difference for the lives of so many people and families.

Designing a new metric to assess belonging

Another area where we believe Anaplan can have a broader influence is in using our platform to enable more sophisticated measurement of the employee experience. We have committed to creating and publishing a new kind of qualitative assessment that analyzes the intersection of diversity, inclusion, and employee sentiment. Taking inspiration from the ubiquitous NPS instrument—net promoter score, which asks the question: "As a consumer, would you recommend this brand?"—we're going deeper. If an organization achieves meaningful diversity in its ranks and intentionally builds an inclusive culture, a sense of belonging should be the outcome. We're thinking of it as a *belonging index* that explores: "As an employee, do you feel like you belong at this company?"

This new metric aims to get to the heart of whether employees feel like they can be their authentic selves and succeed at a company. Do you as a gay man feel like you can be "out" at this company? Do you as a woman feel like you have an equal chance at success as a man? Do you as a Black person feel like your identity is embraced? If you exist at the intersection of several identities, do you feel seen and heard? While we can easily measure diversity in terms of representation, there's currently no good survey or measurement of belonging out there, and we are hoping to fill that gap. This is where most companies struggle: on measuring the actual experience of people from diverse backgrounds and if they feel included and like they belong. Diversity by the numbers is not enough; we need to make sure they succeed and advance and are retained, and the belonging index can help with that.

Our intention is to use the results of the Anaplan *belonging index* to assess more meaningfully how we can improve employee engagement. We will invite other leading companies to join us in using the assessment, which will allow us to benchmark and further refine the tool. My hope is that in this way we'll improve how organizations create inclusion and belonging for *every* employee.

Attract and Retain People

Just as successfully navigating environmental, social, and governance (ESG) issues can attract values-aligned people to your organization, not paying attention to ESG issues can have the opposite effect—it can repel or alienate prospective employees, customers, or stakeholders. Here's an example. Just when you think you've left the Madison Avenue "Mad Men" business culture far behind in your rearview mirror, a story comes along that makes you wonder if you just stepped out of a time machine set to the early 1960s. This was my impression after reading Kara Swisher's *New York Times* column about Pinterest's "culture of discrimination," and its offline character.[7]

Françoise Brougher, the ex-Pinterest executive whose post triggered Swisher's column, said:

> Although 70 percent of Pinterest's users are women, the company is steered by men with little input from female executives. Pinterest's female executives, even at the highest levels, are marginalized, excluded, and silenced. I know because until my firing in April, I was Pinterest's chief operating officer.[8]

In her *Medium* post, Brougher says that in less than two years after she was hired as Pinterest's first COO in March 2018, she was responsible for more than doubling the company's revenue (from $500 million to $1.1 billion), growing Pinterest's base of advertisers from 10,000 to 80,000, and expanding the company's operations to 20 countries. Says Brougher, half of the company's total headcount of 1,500 people reported to her.

According to Brougher, the reason given for her April 2020 dismissal from Pinterest was that she was not being "collaborative." She claims, however, this wasn't the real reason for her firing. Says Brougher, "I believe I was fired for speaking out about the rampant discrimination, hostile work environment, and misogyny that permeates Pinterest."[9]

In August 2020, Brougher sued her former employer "to hold Pinterest accountable and thereby to change its culture."[10]

In her *New York Times* column, Swisher reported that Pinterest's culture was "profoundly dysfunctional," and that she heard stories of gender exclusion from other female Pinterest employees and their former colleagues. According to Swisher, these stories echoed many of the same words over and over: "Sidelined. Shut down. Doors closed. Inner circles. Toxic secrecy. Homegrown boys club. Left out of meetings. Out of key decisions. Out of promotions. Out."[11]

In December 2020, Brougher entered into a stunning $22.5 million settlement from Pinterest. As part of the settlement, Pinterest and Brougher will jointly donate $2.5 million to organizations that support women and underrepresented minorities in tech, with a focus on education, funding, and advocacy.[12] In this case, Pinterest paid a high reputational as well as financial price for its offline character.

The promise of inclusion is that all people can bring incredible value to our collective work. Teams and organizations are better and stronger when we have inclusion and all dimensions of diversity—identity, background, and life experience. Beliefs alone aren't enough—leaders must put our beliefs into action if we want to attract and retain the very best people.

When I became CEO of Anaplan, there were very few women in leadership positions at the company. Unfortunately, like so many Silicon Valley companies, the Anaplan culture at the time was shaped and filtered by white-male experiences and perspectives.

While we still have much more work to do, we have made great progress increasing strong female leadership. We now have three women on our board of directors—Brooke Major-Reid, who is also our first Black board member, joined us in late 2020. Women hold key executive positions and VP-level roles leading Anaplan's Engineering, Strategy, Human Resources, Marketing, Culture and Communications, Commercial Solutions, Sales, Finance, and many other functions. These very talented women are highly visible leaders across the organization, and Anaplan is a better, more successful organization because of their decision-making, strategic thinking, and management capability.

To support this ongoing effort to make our workforce more diverse, we belong to the Paradigm for Parity coalition—a group of business leaders, board members, and academics who are committed to a goal of gender parity by 2030. As a member of this coalition, we have made a commitment to adopt a clear plan of action that drives impact, and we have mutual accountability for measurable results.[13] The Paradigm for Parity Action Plan has five components that all member organizations must adopt:

1. Minimize or Eliminate Unconscious Bias
2. Significantly Increase the Number of Women in Senior Operating Roles
3. Measure Targets at Every Level and Communicate Progress and Results Regularly
4. Base Career Progress on Business Results and Performance, Not Presence
5. Identify Women of Potential and Give Them Sponsors as Well as Mentors[14]

We are committed to attracting and retaining a diverse group of people with character. We have launched Textio, an augmented-writing platform, to make our job descriptions and recruiter outreach more inclusive. Its artificial intelligence generates and suggests language that engages passive candidates and attracts job seekers. We also hired Recruiting Toolbox to conduct behavior-based training meant to help interviewers and hiring managers define their hiring criteria, interview effectively, and make the right hiring decisions. In addition, all people leaders at Anaplan are required to complete unconscious bias training that focuses on hiring, team dynamics, career growth, and how to create a culture of belonging.

Unconscious bias is powerfully insidious. No company should willingly exclude anyone from key decision roles in an organization simply because he or she isn't the "right" gender or race or any other factor that has nothing to do with someone's talent and worth as a person. It just doesn't make sense. Yet it still happens. It is imperative for leaders to actively engage—in whatever ways are right for their business and industry and stakeholders—in assessing hiring practices and driving better ways to identify, recruit, develop, and retain diverse talent. Most important, we've got to actively seek people who are different from ourselves, and work to overcome biases that have long fostered homogenous workplaces.

Matthew Jordan is an Employee Communications Associate at Anaplan. After graduating from university, he did some contract writing, but found the constant grind of deadlines and lack of interaction as a remote worker unsatisfying. Says Jordan, "I felt like I was a cog in the machine at my previous job. There was no real personal connection to what I was writing, which inevitably led to me feeling burned out."[15]

He started looking for something new, but after several months was beginning to feel discouraged. Although he's a talented writer and conscientious worker, job hunting was incredibly stressful because Jordan has Asperger's. People with this condition are often very knowledgeable about specific interests and high functioning in life and work, but have difficulty with social interaction. One-on-one interviews are particularly challenging because of the expectation to make eye contact and speak confidently about oneself.

Jordan came to Anaplan as a contractor on the Employee Communications team. He quickly proved himself as a focused writer and contributor and converted to a full-time role. Over time, he opened up and talked about his neurodiversity—a part of his identity that he'd previously kept hidden. Being open about it has helped his team understand that he expresses himself differently and responds best to specific questions—and although he's quiet in a group, he has strong opinions, expertise, and a wicked sense of humor.

Another example that shows open-mindedness paying off involves a young man with an unconventional hiring story. In 2018, Daanish Soomar was job hunting in Minneapolis and getting nothing but rejections. Inspired by a story he read on LinkedIn, he decided to try something completely different. Soomar went to the Minneapolis Skyway (in the middle of the business district) with 100 copies of his resume and a cardboard sign that read: "On a mission: launch career, take a resume." He got the attention of someone at Anaplan who was impressed with his creativity and tenacity, which landed him a job with the company as a product support analyst.

The story doesn't end there. After developing his skills at Anaplan for two years with support from his mentors, Soomar now serves as an Anaplan analyst with one of our consulting partners, Slalom. For us, this is a happy ending—when people can leverage their Anaplan expertise for further professional growth, it strengthens the Anaplan brand and the overall ecosystem. We are proud to see the ranks of Anaplan users continue to grow both inside our organization and throughout the business community.

When you hire people across all dimensions of diversity yet with aligned values, the difference to the employee experience is profound. We collaborate well. We have fun at work. We help each other. We trust each other. We can disagree and move on, working toward the same goals. And we manifest the company character we hope to achieve. Make no mistake about it—creating a culture that is diverse and inclusive, and maintaining and strengthening it over time, is not easy and it is not without challenge. But it provides us with a framework to forge our way through difficult moments.

And it attracts people of character—the kind of people we all want to work with.

Hiring for Character

Building an inclusive workplace filled with people of character requires a very thoughtful and intentional hiring process. At Anaplan, we look for people who are collaborative and enjoy solving challenging problems in a fast-changing, dynamic environment. And because our core values are key to everything we do, the talented people we recruit must not only be skilled at their jobs, they must also exemplify our values every day of the week. We want people who are creative, tenacious, and authentic, and who think big and act bold. This is true for *every* employee—including the C-suite.

Consider the example from the previous chapter of the executive who had passed all the interview criteria and was just a step away from being hired onto the leadership team of the Walt Disney Company. That is, he was until he balked at the idea of parking strollers during the course of his culture interview. That lost him the job because he demonstrated that he was not a fit with the Disney culture.

When you hire, retain, and promote employees with upstanding character—at every level, from top to bottom—you create a virtuous circle, attracting other people with character. And when you don't, you run the risk of driving them away. One leader I interviewed told me about an executive who was a net negative to the organization. Despite his strong business performance, he displayed terrible character. It worked for a while—until it didn't, creating a fearful culture that ultimately backfired. According to this executive:

> Before [the new CEO] took charge, there was a president in the U.S. business unit who was absolutely terrifying but had been extremely successful hitting business goals, being very ambitious, and turning around the business units. He was assigned to the U.S. business to turn it around. He would make people cry in meetings. He would berate people and attack them on a personal level—creating an incredible culture of fear.

And guess what would happen in that environment? There was so much fear that we would waste time practicing and having pre- pre- pre- pre-meetings, and writing scripts. I was taking zero risks and trying to second-guess what that president would want to hear rather than being free to think and be creative. It created a terrible, scary culture. Despite his high performance, this sort of behavior was unsustainable in our current culture, and he's now gone.[16]

In a survey of more than 10,000 Millennials conducted by PwC, more than 80 percent of respondents said that an employer's policy on diversity, equality, and workforce inclusion is an important factor in their decision about whether to work for the company. According to PwC:

This reflects people's desire to be part of a business that not only offers them opportunities to develop their individual careers, but also has values which are aligned to their own. When this policy resonates with the brand, it can form a key component of the employee value proposition (EVP)—why people would want to work for the organization.[17]

In essence, your business becomes a magnet for people of character. I asked Yvonne Wassenaar how she hires for character—more specifically, what she looks for in a job candidate. Said Wassenaar:

There are some fundamental things that I look for when I interview. I look for resiliency. I don't look for people who always got it right—I look for people who have been willing to take risks and are comfortable talking about their failures as learning experiences. I look for references. And, particularly in leaders, I ask myself, "Who are the people that will follow this individual, and why?"[18]

Culture isn't just about what a company says its values are; it's communicated in subtle ways too, like the atmosphere when you walk into an office. When you bring someone in for an interview, they can immediately pick up on what kind of company you are, what your values are, and the culture you have created. YY Lee, Anaplan's Chief Strategy Officer, told us about her experience interviewing at another company she ultimately felt wasn't aligned with her own values. Here's the story she told me about this experience:

I was recruited by an organization for a role that would be the gold star on any career—the kind of position that very, very few people get offered. The role had a "C" in front of it and the compensation they offered was just unreal. So, we're having these conversations and literally everybody there is just absolutely brilliant, interesting, terrific, and high performing.

They showed me where my office would be. It was in a row of other offices—all mahogany paneling with glass and steel. Really beautiful. When I walked into the office that would be mine, there was a full view of San Francisco Bay and the Bay Bridge through the large glass windows. Outside of each office was a cubicle, and inside each cubicle sat a female executive assistant. Most of the offices were empty, but even so, the executive assistants weren't talking to one another. They were just quietly sitting there—waiting for something to happen.

"I can't be here," I said to myself. I would have had one of those beautiful offices, the Bay Bridge view, the executive assistant who would sit quietly there, whether I was in the office or not. This company was so clearly about status and trappings and exalting the senior-most ranks of their leadership. They were more about hierarchy than they were about collaboration. Up until then, I had the best conversations with some very smart people. But when I walked down that hallway, I just knew at that very moment that we would have our meeting and I would politely decline the offer. I'm out—we're done.[19]

When you're hiring for character, you'll be showcasing your own. Upstanding character prioritizes inclusion and collaboration, and as a leader you have to ensure experiences and impressions live up to intentions. When you model upstanding character, you'll get more of it in return—and you'll attract and retain the kind of people you want in your organization.

Evaluating Talent for Character

In any job interview, you will, of course, want to get to the heart of a candidate's actual work skills. If you're interviewing for a product manager, for example, you'll want to ask detailed questions about his or her experience leading a product team. If you're interviewing an accounts payable clerk, you'll want to ask detailed questions about his or her experience in accounting. And, if you're hiring a graphic designer, you'll want to ask detailed questions about his or her experience in that.

But, what about their values? How can you determine what kind of core values the job candidate believes in, and whether this person is going to be a good fit with your own organization's core values and culture?

What you can do is set aside time in the interview to ask values-based questions that will help you determine in advance candidates' values and behaviors, and the kind of culture and team environment they most prefer to work in. Ultimately, you'll want to learn more about their integrity, personal responsibility and accountability, and dedication to their team and organization. You'll want to gauge how adaptable and collaborative they will be, how innovative they are, the extent of their customer focus, and if they are good communicators—both inside and outside the organization.

Key to asking effective interview questions is making sure they are open-ended, not the kind that can be answered with a simple "yes" or "no." You want your job candidates to provide you with in-depth answers and examples from their personal experience that will help you better understand how they will react when they have opportunities or problems to deal with in your own organization. The best way to understand these nuances is to ask your candidates to tell you a story.

For example, Julie Zhuo, cofounder of tech advisory firm Inspirit and former VP Product Design for Facebook, suggests asking the question, "Imagine yourself in three years. What do you hope will be different about you then compared to now?" Explains Zhuo, "Asking a candidate to describe her vision for her own growth in the next three years helps me understand the candidate's ambitions as well as how goal-oriented and self-reflective she is."[20]

Alyssa Henry, Head of Seller & Developer Business Units & Infrastructure Engineering for Square, suggests this question: "Tell me about your ideal next role. What characteristics does it have from a responsibility, team, and company culture perspective? What characteristics does it not have?" Says Henry, "This two-part question helps determine if there's a match in expectations for the role. Particularly when you hear the answers to what they're not looking for, sometimes you realize that the candidate is actually a better match for a different role." She continues, "But my favorite part is that it gives you the selling points you need to hit on when it comes time to close the candidate. You already know what they value, which makes it easier to tailor your pitch."[21]

And Cristina Cordova, Head of Platform & Partnerships at Notion, likes to ask this three-part question: "Tell me about a time you strongly disagreed with your manager. What did you do to convince him or her that you were right? What ultimately happened?" According to Cordova, the answer she gets from the interviewee "shows me how far someone will go in order to do what they believe is right. The way candidates choose to unpack the anecdote also shows me how they convince others in the face of obstacles. Do they use data? Do they gather support from others?" She also finds value in the ultimate resolution of the disagreement: "How they speak about not getting their way tells you a lot about whether they're willing to disagree and commit to execution."[22]

Says Laszlo Bock, former SVP of People Operations for Google and CEO and cofounder of Humu:

> Behavioral interviewing also works—where you're not giving someone a hypothetical, but you're starting with a question like, "Give me an example of a time when you solved an analytically difficult problem." The interesting thing about the behavioral interview is that when you ask somebody to speak to their own experience, and you drill into that, you get two kinds of information. One is you get to see how they actually interacted in a real-world situation, and the valuable "meta" information you get about the candidate is a sense of what they consider to be difficult.[23]

Here are some examples of values-based questions that will help you determine whether a candidate is a fit for your organization's core values and culture:

- Tell me about a time you had a conflict with a coworker. What was the conflict about and how did you resolve it?
- What do you do to keep morale up on your team?
- How did you deal with a coworker you didn't get along with?
- What is your life's purpose and how do you bring that to your work?
- How did you handle an employee who disagreed with your evaluation of their work performance?
- What's one example of how you solved a difficult problem in a unique way?
- Tell me about a time when you showed compassion to a coworker who was in a difficult situation.
- Teach me something.
- Do you think it's better for a delivery to be perfect but late, or imperfect but on time? Explain your reasoning.

- Describe how you handled a disagreement with a key customer.
- What events in your life have had the greatest impact on the person you are today?
- How did you handle a situation when you were late for an important deadline?
- Tell me something you have taught yourself in the last six months.
- What would your current manager tell me makes you most valuable to them?
- How do you go about deciding whether an idea is worth pursuing?
- One year from now, how will you judge whether your time with our company has been a success?

When you ask values-based questions such as these, look for responses that are clearly in opposition to your organization's core values and culture. Then look for inconsistencies in the candidate's responses. If, for example, the candidate says that he is "creative and innovative," but can't provide you with specific examples of being creative and innovative on the job, then that's a red flag. And always watch for signs that the candidate thinks she is better than everyone else—that the world revolves around her. While someone may be well qualified for the work he or she does, arrogance will quickly destroy relationships on the team.

Some interviewers like to use "brainteaser" questions meant to put job candidates on the spot to see how they react or to put their creativity to the test. While the responses can be interesting, it's hard to draw conclusions about a candidate's character or values based on them. Here's a sample brainteaser interview question reportedly used by a popular computer manufacturer:

> There are three boxes, one contains only apples, one contains only oranges, and one contains both apples and oranges. The boxes have been incorrectly labeled such that no label identifies the actual contents of its box. Opening just one box, and without looking in the box, you take out one piece of fruit. By looking at the fruit, how can you immediately label all of the boxes correctly?[24]

Says Bock about this kind of interview question:

> On the hiring side, we found that brainteasers are a complete waste of time. How many golf balls can you fit into an airplane? How many

gas stations in Manhattan? A complete waste of time. They don't predict anything. They serve primarily to make the interviewer feel smart. Instead, what works well are structured behavioral interviews, where you have a consistent rubric for how you assess people, rather than having each interviewer just make stuff up.[25]

That said, it can be helpful to ask the occasional curveball question that is unexpected and causes your interviewees to think beyond their pre-rehearsed and pat answers and responses. For example, Romy Macasieb—Principal Product Manager at Livongo—has this favorite curveball question: "Why shouldn't we hire you?" Says Macasieb, "It goes much deeper than your standard 'What are your three areas of improvement?' type questions. I like that it allows interviewees to play both sides of the table. They could highlight the skills they're missing or why they might not be what we're looking for by saying something like 'You shouldn't hire me if you want someone that is quant-only.'" Macasieb continues, "But they can also turn the focus to why you might not be a fit for them. I've heard responses like 'You shouldn't hire me if you have an open office floor plan.'"[26]

Linda Lee is Anaplan's Vice President, Executive Communications and Culture. Before she conducts an interview, she does extensive research on the individual so that she can tailor context-based questions that are very specific to that person. In addition, Lee has a very finely tuned set of general questions—developed over years of interviewing—for ferreting out core values and culture fit in job candidates. Here are the general questions she always asks:

- For C-level positions or senior level roles, she reviews the latest headlines related to their expertise, and she questions how they would manage that particular situation. For example, with an HR leader, she asked the question about the Google engineer who questioned women's abilities to become engineers. How would you advise the Google CEO? What would you do with the engineer? How would you address the employee base?
- What is some cringe-worthy feedback you received, and what did you do about it?
- How have you helped advance the careers of others?
- When was the last time you didn't want to work on a project at work, and why?
- What's the one part of your job you wish you could outsource?

- If you vehemently disagreed with a decision by the CEO, what would you do?
- What is your superpower? What can you do that others can rarely do?
- How have your hobbies helped you at work?
- What's the one question you wished I asked?
- What's the one question you are glad I didn't ask?

Before you interview a prospective new employee, be sure to do your homework and go beyond the usual questions that everyone always asks. Make a point of getting to the heart of whether the person in front of you (or on the videoconference screen) is a person of character and will be a good match for your culture. Taking the time up front to do this may save you hours of aggravation later on if you end up hiring the wrong person.

Building an Upstanding Leadership Team

When you're building a team of upstanding leaders, ask yourself, "How do we get at the heart of their character, are we asking the right questions?" If we're not, then we've got to think through the process, come up with better questions, and take the time now versus after someone is hired. Sue Bostrom serves on a number of tech company boards, including Anaplan's, where she is chair of the compensation committee. I asked her to tell me what she looks for when interviewing prospective leaders. She said:

> What are their leadership stories? What risks have they been willing to take? Will they be someone who will sit around the executive table and say, "Hey, you know what, Frank? That is not the right thing for us to do—I don't feel comfortable with it." Do they have a history of standing up for what is right and challenging the status quo in a positive, productive way?
>
> Another area to explore when you're recruiting executives is to gauge their inclination toward continuous learning. Do we hire leaders who realize that the world is always changing, and that we always have to be learning, growing, and evolving? Do we lean into the tough questions to make sure that we're hiring people like that?[27]

Bostrom often conducts evaluations of CEOs of the companies where she's on the board. Here's her perspective on what she observes, both good and bad. Note that this advice applies to more than just the CEO level in the organization:

> I've heard it said that every CEO, to have the determination to become a CEO, has a "flaw." The questions are: What is that flaw, how big is it, and how much will it really impact the daily lives of employees and the ability of the company to be successful?
>
> I try to identify CEO flaws, and there's no shame because we've all got them. Sometimes it's an Achilles heel, a strength we overuse so that it actually becomes a weakness. For example, you might be overly loyal to employees who you have worked with for a long time and struggle to objectively assess their performance. Ideally, the board and I work with the CEO on areas for improvement to optimize his/her effectiveness and the company's ability to be successful.[28]

Finally, you want to identify leaders who value the team they're playing for. Bostrom reminded me about a story that Coach K—Mike Krzyzewski, the head men's basketball coach at Duke University—once told us when we were both executives at Cisco. Bostrom recounted the story:

> In basketball, you play for the name on the front of the jersey (the team), not for the name on the back of the jersey (your name). It's the philosophy that you put the company first and yourself second. An interesting question is, where do we put our community in that list of priorities? The whole idea of social responsibility—what exactly does that mean for companies today?
>
> My feeling is that social responsibility is not so much about checking a box for investors—it's about who we are as a company. What do we think is in the best interest of our community and what we stand for? And, also, what's good for the business? Because, when you intersect all these areas, it's really easy to do the right thing—and create a win-win for the community and the company.[29]

There's something else we do to build strong, upstanding leadership and other teams in Anaplan, and that's to use a personality assessment called the True Tilt Personality Profile (Tilt365 for short),[30] which I learned about at Red Hat. We used it with great success in Finance, Operations, IT, and in a few other areas of the Red Hat organization. There are many personality assessments out there, and every company has its favorites. However, I have found that Tilt365 really gets to the heart of what makes people tick and can be a very helpful tool for shaping team culture. And at Anaplan, we have definitely taken it to a whole new level.

The Tilt365 assessment provides people with a profile of their work style, clearly indicating their natural character strengths, and also the kinds of people they work well with, and those who are a challenge for them to work with. What I appreciate about Tilt365 is that every person has all four personality types; we just tend to lean toward one or two more than the rest. Tilt365 categorizes people into four main personality Tilting patterns:

- **The Cross Pollinator.** People who Tilt toward Connection are focused on connecting People and Ideas—their top character strengths are seen as Likability, Empathy, Inspiration, and Openness. They are quick and spontaneous, and they want freedom and diplomacy from others. When under stress, they may become overwhelmed and confused. Their motto is "So many ideas, so many people, so little time."
- **The Change Catalyst.** People who Tilt toward Impact are focused on connecting Ideas and Action—their top character strengths are Confidence, Creativity, Boldness, and Inspiration. They are naturals at inventing new solutions and innovating and they want to change the world. They may feel anger and frustration when under stress, and their motto is "Everything that tests me makes me feel alive!"
- **The Quiet Genius.** People who Tilt toward Clarity are focused on connecting People and Data, and their top character strengths are seen as Trust, Perspective, Empathy, and Focus. Quiet Geniuses interpret and analyze data that affect people—they are not ready to make decisions quite yet. They want to investigate the details first. They default to resistance when under stress and their motto is "It's better to prepare than to regret."
- **The Master Mind.** People who Tilt toward Structure are focused on connecting Data and Results. Their top character strengths are Diligence, Integrity, Focus, and Boldness. They are focused on execution and building intricate, precise systems that offer stability and scalability over time. When under stress, they tend to obsess and micromanage. Their motto is "Efficiency and precision is perfection."

When someone has developed balance in all the character traits of the Tilt365 model, they are able to lean into whichever trait is necessary in a given situation. This person is known as *The Positive Influencer*—the epitome of Tilt365. They balance taking action with consideration of others, and they balance innovation with grounded thinking. In addition, they exhibit the overarching meta-strength of agility, which is important today in terms of what the whole-person development enables. Their motto is "Be Kind, Be Wise, Be Bold, Be Unique, Be Real."[31]

The Tilt framework of 12 key character strengths and 4 meta-strengths: resilience, courage, wisdom, and humanity

Credit: Tilt365 Framework of 12 Character Strengths and Personas developed by Pam Boney from www.tilt365.com. © 2020 Tilt, Inc.

All Anaplan employees—current and new—go through Tilt365 assessment and training. When we know where we come from as far as the different character traits in Tilt365; we understand what makes us tick and what creates challenges. It allows us to understand each other better and find ways to get to work better together—and ultimately gets us faster to win/win relationships.

When we went through the Tilt365 assessments at the executive level, we were surprised at how many of us Tilted toward Structure. Organizations experiencing hypergrowth want a lot of Impact and Structure in their executive teams, and the Tilt365 assessment can help in achieving this through thoughtful hiring practices.

For character and diversity in an organization, you need to have a range of Tilting patterns. Having all Structures in your organization, or having all Impacts, won't get you where you want to go. Tilt365 helps create diversity by forcing the right balance. It's a way to continue to navigate as a company and to make sure you're getting the right perspectives.

Not only does every new hire get training right away, we also provide our executive team and senior leaders with training every year. We trained internal employees to be our Tilt365 facilitators across the company, and we encourage our teams to provide Tilt365 training on a regular basis, especially if new people join so you can understand your Team Tilting profile. What I appreciate about Tilt365 is that you can't help but confirm so many things about yourself. When you read your report, it's uncanny how accurate it is about you.

However, my favorite part about Tilt365 is learning about the other personality patterns and understanding how or why others react a certain way. It offers you empathy, understanding, and awareness, and now that you know better, you react better. Many times, in our executive team meetings, an executive will call out his or her Tilt, acknowledging that he or she may be focused on efficiency or a risk, or we will call out to someone based on his or her Tilt perspective to ensure we have thought through everything. It's a simple but powerful tool to ensure all voices are heard and people feel valued.

Like the majority of CEOs, I Tilt to Impact, the **Change Catalyst**, and my No. 1 irritant is negativity. I need to see the positive and optimistic side of the story with people I'm working with. If someone is constantly pessimistic with me, that frustrates me. That doesn't force me to ignore the negative side because I want to get all perspectives—it's not "see no evil, hear no evil, speak no evil." It's the knowledge that I Tilt that way, which helps me remember that others Tilt differently. Once I know someone's Tilt, it allows me to lean in toward that part of my personality so we can get the results we need.

Where Tilt365 is most effective depends on the situation you're in. For example, when I am preparing for a major speaking engagement such as our annual user conference—Connected Planning Xperience (CPX)— I will consult various strong Tilts from across the company to get their points of view. A **Cross Pollinator** will want to hear the stories about the people related to planning. A **Quiet Genius** will want to understand the how, where, when, and why of what I am talking about—the context and details. A **Master Mind** wants me to get on with it and be clear about the results, outcomes, and solutions we can provide for them efficiently. Finally, a **Change Catalyst** is looking for my leadership and strategy—the big picture—to determine if I am being bold enough. If I can resonate with all four Tilts, then I know I will capture the attention of the majority of my audience with my keynote.

Building an organization and a culture of upstanding character requires recruiting, hiring, and retaining people of upstanding character. As leaders, it's our job to ensure that we find ways to attract a diverse group of people and then include them in every aspect of what we do. Only when people feel like they belong will they trust the organization and those who they work for and with, and give the very best of themselves. We must create an environment that makes this the default experience and not the exception.

PART III

Putting Character into Action

CHAPTER 8

Responding to Crisis

"The Chinese use two brush strokes to write the word 'crisis.' One brush stroke stands for danger; the other for opportunity."

—John F. Kennedy

Your true character is what shows up in times of crisis.

No matter what kind of organization you work for, your company will be tested and pushed to its limits by crisis. Whether it's company-specific (when Volkswagen was caught cheating on emissions standards), regionally based (the 2011 earthquake, tsunami, and Fukushima nuclear disaster in Japan), or global in scope (the 2008 financial crisis), it's rare for any organization to escape the blistering heat of crisis. The question is not *if* it will happen, but *when*.

The night after the murder of George Floyd in May 2020, protests against police brutality began in Minneapolis then spread quickly to other U.S. cities, and eventually, worldwide. I had posted a short note on Slack expressing support for Black Lives Matter and the Black community, and we held our all-company meeting a week after the protests broke out.

Every minute that I wasn't in meetings, I was reading the news and educating myself about the rampant racism and inequity that Black communities have had to endure. I was disturbed and saddened, but also filled with resolve about what I needed to do as a concerned citizen, parent, and CEO. Although the all-company meeting helped to set the tone for internal discussions, two things happened that felt like a punch in the gut.

When we initially heard about the protests happening in Minneapolis, we sent a note to our employees there offering whatever help they might need. In the moment, this felt like the right thing to do. The following week, we convened a small group of our Black employees to listen to their concerns and solicit their feedback. In that session, one woman expressed her disappointment that we didn't reach out to check in and offer our support for Black employees across the company, the ones who were traumatized by George Floyd's murder and the ongoing racism and injustice in our society. We had directed our sympathy to employees who were afraid of disruption and disorder in their city, instead of prioritizing our own Black community, for whom the protests resonated as a way to express justified anger and grief. People in the Black community, and our Black employees, specifically, needed support and empathy most of all.

Did we demonstrate character in this moment of crisis? We were under pressure to act quickly and did what we thought was right at the time, but we fell short. Having upstanding character doesn't mean you will always be right about every situation, but it does require the ability to be introspective, and to learn from mistakes.

The lesson here was twofold: We implemented what we thought was the right response, without checking in with our Black employees. We've since had several meetings with our Black employee resource group, and one of their key points of advice to us was "Always ask; don't assume." Before rolling out a communication or policy that impacts any marginalized community, we must get the feedback of its community members to hear directly what their concerns are instead of assuming we know.

The second lesson is that it's hard to have that built-in gut check if your leadership team is missing that representation. Our executive team at Anaplan is quite diverse—six out of nine were born outside the United States; four out of nine are women; and three out of nine are people of color. But we don't (yet) have a Black executive in the top ranks of the company, and it's something I regret. And I say that not to excuse our decisions, but to emphasize that this is an example where we are losing out by missing that perspective on the executive team.

Another challenging situation that week was when an employee posted a long rebuttal to my Slack post about how he did not see the point of the Black Lives Matter movement, and that the problem in Minneapolis could be solved through action against the officers involved without reference to racism. I was in back-to-back meetings the entire day and did not see this until it had amassed more than 20 replies and numerous counter-posts from employees across the company who respectfully challenged the original poster (OP) and explained why his point of view was not only wrong but incredibly hurtful. The OP doubled down on his statement by directly reply-ing to almost everyone in the thread with the same message, creating chaos in the online forum.

A couple of points stood out from the Slack discussion. First, I was incredibly proud that so many Anaplan employees chimed in respectfully and made the effort to educate the OP and explain why racism is inextri-cable from police brutality in the United States, and why everyone needs to take a stance on this. These supportive responses came from all parts of the company—many of the posters were white, some from Europe and England, and some were people of color. I was encouraged by this show of allyship.

Reading through the responses, I was glad to see the level of transpar-ency and dialogue that our employees achieved without any facilitation or monitoring. It gave me hope that I was not alone in trying to educate myself and be more vocal about racial justice and how to become a more inclusive organization—many employees already shared this view and were empowered to speak up.

The second point I noticed is that there were almost no replies or responses from Black employees, except one that said, "I hate how small and vulnerable the Black community feels at Anaplan and how none of us feel safe to comment on the all-company meeting and [OP]'s post." That one poignant, vulnerable statement got to the heart of the issue: We were still talking "around" the Black employees and not with them, and they did not feel safe commenting publicly when someone like the OP could post something so ignorant and defensive and seem to get away with it. The Black employee was flooded with supportive responses (both pub-licly and privately). But this made me realize that even though Anaplan is full of people who value diversity and exemplify our core values, we still have work to do to make our workplace even more representative and inclusive.

We followed up with a variety of actions internally and externally, including holding focus groups with Black employees, starting the BEAD (Black Employees of African Descent) employee resource group, invit-ing guest speakers to company-wide meetings about anti-racism, rolling out unconscious bias training, and retaining a consultant and facilitator as noted in Chapter 7 to work with our leadership team. We've made a con-certed effort to prioritize and listen to Black voices within our company and seek outside experts to share their knowledge with us—and to hold us accountable.

I've noticed an interesting inflection point during the course of 2020: CEOs became much more courageous in taking stands on the core values that they and their organizations live by. Many are making a real effort to show employees, customers, shareholders, and other stakeholders—and the communities in which they do business—that they and their organizations have upstanding character, that they are willing to take sometimes unpopular stands and then defend them, and that they use their core values to guide their decisions, often in very public ways.

Consider the example of Amazon CEO Jeff Bezos. In the wake of the George Floyd killing and the resulting wave of protests that swept the nation, Amazon placed this banner prominently at the top of its home page:

Black lives matter

Amazon stands in solidarity

with the Black community

Perhaps it's no surprise that not every Amazon customer was happy to see the company declare its support for the Black Lives Matter movement. One customer, Macy, took the time to write Bezos a personal email—with the subject line "All Lives Matter"—expressing her personal concerns:

It is quite disturbing to get on the Amazon website and see "BLACK LIVES MATTER."

You provide services to more than millions of people. Including myself and the rest of my family for our business needs and personal purchases. I am for everyone voicing their opinions and standing up for what you believe in, but for your company to blast this on your website is very offensive to me and I'm sure you'll be hearing from others. **ALL LIVES MATTER!**

And if it wasn't for all these lives providing their service for you and your company, where would Amazon be today?

Bezos shared the email (with Macy's last name redacted) on his Instagram page on June 5, along with his response back to Macy:

No, Macy, I have to disagree with you. "Black lives matter" doesn't mean other lives don't matter. Black lives matter speaks to racism and the disproportionate risk that Black people face in our law enforcement and justice system. I have a 20-year-old son, and I simply don't worry that he might be choked to death while being detained one day. It's not something I worry about. Black parents can't say the same.

None of this is intended to dismiss or minimize the very real worries you or anyone else might have in their own life, but I want you to know I support this movement that we see happening all around us, and my stance won't change.

My sincere very best to you.

Jeff[1]

A couple days later, Bezos shared another, expletive-filled email on Instagram that he received regarding Amazon's stance on Black Lives Matter. At the end of his rant, the author stated that he cancelled his order with Amazon and that his business relationship with the company "is over." I won't reproduce that email here, but suffice it to say that it was appalling. Bezos's response to Dave—the email's author—was direct and unequivocal. In part:

This sort of hate shouldn't be allowed to hide in the shadows. It's important to make it visible. This is just one example of the problem.

And, Dave, you're the kind of customer I'm happy to lose.[2]

In a recent *Harvard Business Review* article, Laysha Ward—Executive Vice President and Chief External Engagement Officer at Target—explained how her company is countering systemic racism with anti-racist business strategies. Target established REACH (Racial Equity Action and Change Committee) to increase Black representation on its teams. Going further, the company is evaluating its foundational purchasing and policy practices for ways to advance racial equity and social justice. Said Ward, "We'll also make changes to the products we sell, our approach to marketing, our community involvement, and how we influence public policy."[3]

Sundar Pichai, CEO of Google and Alphabet, asked employees to stand with him at 1 p.m. on June 3 to "honor the memories of Black lives lost in an 8-minute and 46-second moment of silence."[4] On June 5, Alexis Ohanian, cofounder of Reddit, announced his decision to resign from the Reddit board of directors. Said Ohanian in a post to his personal blog, "I have urged them to fill my seat with a Black candidate...."[5]

Being a company with upstanding character won't necessarily prevent you from experiencing a crisis, but it will give you a solid foundation and set of principles for how you respond to crisis and move forward.

When You Are Called, How Do You Answer?

Every organization has core values, whether or not they are published. And, for the most part, I believe that most leaders do everything they can to live their core values—to walk the talk and to model these behaviors to their people. However, the real test is what leaders do when there's a crisis or some other extreme pressure on the organization.

When you are called to action and the stakes are high, how do you answer?

Do you lean into your core values even harder—using them as guardrails to help guide your decisions and actions—or do you abandon them, rationalizing that you'll circle back to them once the situation calms down?

I suggest that, in crisis, your core values are more important than ever. They are the North Star that shines a steady light on the course you should follow as you navigate through uncertain and disruptive times. In his book *Trailblazer*, Salesforce founder, Chairman, and CEO Marc Benioff says, "Lots of businesses talk about values, but in turbulent times, when they matter most, executives often forget to operationalize them. They see values as expensive luxuries that should remain nailed harmlessly to the wall when making major business decisions."[6]

Values are anything but expensive luxuries, and they should be used and referenced frequently when making major business decisions instead of being forgotten in a picture frame—especially in times of crisis. They are your foundation, your inspiration, your framework for action.

When we are called, how do we answer?

In March 2020—as the COVID-19 global pandemic swept across the United States, CVS Health committed to awarding bonuses to frontline employees "who are required to be at CVS facilities to assist patients and customers in this time of unprecedented need." The recipients of these bonuses—which ranged from $150 to $500—included pharmacists, store managers and associates, and other on-site hourly employees. In addition, the company partnered with Bright Horizons to provide employees with up to 25 fully covered days of backup care for children or adult dependents, and it offered 14 days of paid sick leave to any employee—full- or part-time—who tested positive for COVID-19.[7]

And when CVS Health needed to hire 50,000 new employees in the "most ambitious hiring drive in the company's history" to fill these positions, they reached out to a list of more than 60 clients and partner organizations that had furloughed or laid off workers. This list included Marriott and Hilton, which had both been forced to furlough workers as people dramatically cut back on their travel plans in the wake of the pandemic.[8]

LVMH—the conglomerate that includes luxury brands such as Givenchy and Christian Dior—switched its manufacturing facilities from producing perfumes and cosmetics to making hand sanitizer, which was then donated to French health authorities at no cost.[9] Cisco made a commitment to donate $210 million worth of technology services to business and governments; UberEats donated free rides and food to beleaguered healthcare workers and first responders; Airbnb provided free accommodation to healthcare workers who traveled to COVID-19 hotspots; Netflix established a $100 million fund to help support out-of-work TV and film cast and crew; and JetBlue, Delta, and United Airlines offered to let medical workers fly for free.[10] The list goes on and on.

Through our Anaplan Helps initiative, Anaplan offered its services to organizations responding to the pandemic, including a free trial of our platform. More than 20 free downloadable applications were created for organizations to manage complex tasks, including hospital staffing, predicting demand for hospital beds and equipment based on public health data, allocating scarce supplies of personal protective equipment (PPE), matching volunteers with vulnerable people in their neighborhoods, and helping restaurants pivot to food delivery.

We also prioritized our employees' safety and well-being by communicating frequently, promoting mental health resources, offering a stipend to purchase home office/ergonomic equipment for working at home, and giving Well Being Days off (nine additional company-wide holidays in 2020) to ensure everyone was getting enough rest and time to recharge. At a time when many companies were having to furlough or lay off employees, we maintained our staffing, continued to hire for open roles, and offered equity grants to invest in our employees and show our appreciation.

The response from employees was overwhelming—and personally gratifying to me and the rest of the executive team. We conducted a survey after the FAQ company-wide meeting where we announced how we will support employees with extra flexibility during our extended period of working from home, and we've never had so many responses and such positive feedback to a post-event survey. People were not only pleased with the new programs, but they felt we had provided them with real peace of mind during these very uncertain times. As one employee put it, "I will fight like heck on behalf of Anaplan because you are taking care of me beyond what I expected. This has elevated my relationship with Anaplan beyond just being a transactional employee. This is muscle memory for the future because you will have this deeply loyal group of employees who will do anything for Anaplan."

Every company has had to deal with the effects of the COVID-19 global pandemic in its own unique way. We are no exception. Fortunately, like most technology companies, we were able to transition to working from home very quickly. But making this shift brought about all sorts of challenges that we had to work through as we did our best to maintain our employees' well-being and business continuity.

Marilyn Miller, Chief People Officer at Anaplan, was instrumental in helping us work through this momentous transition guided by our values. Says Miller about our approach to COVID-19:

> I witnessed the company continue to work through the COVID-19 situation, and I watched the completeness and the thoughtfulness by which we've navigated this—key has been staying in constant communication with our employees and approaching it from multiple dimensions. How do we educate our people? How do we keep people safe? How do we make decisions and how do we articulate those decisions? Some decisions we know are going to be popular, and some decisions we knew would be met with angst. But the way that we are staying in communication with our people, in full transparency and revealing what was behind the decision-making, I think is a real testament to the culture and the character of the company.

> We give choice where we were able to, and we make decisions where we feel we need to. I think the sentiment coming from employees in terms of the way that we navigate all of that, is a true test of character. We never lose sight of the fact that employee safety and well-being, and then continuing to enable our customers and have business continuity, all have to be priorities. Not always equally, and not always at the same time. There are times we emphasize safety, and there are times when we emphasize ensuring our customers are getting what they need.

There is truth to the fact that the business has to be successful to keep our people employed. And while that is a big aspect of it, we have to do it safely and thoughtfully.[11]

Ultimately, I believe that's the balance we, as leaders, must always keep in mind as we make important, sometimes life-changing, decisions. We must always take care of our employees while ensuring that we maintain a strong customer focus. And faced with uncertainty or crisis, we must make decisions that are consistent with our beliefs and that we know we can look back on later without regret.

Crises are true tests of an organization's character and values—I'm convinced that those with upstanding character and strong values are better able to weather the storm than those that do not have a strong foundation of character and values. A crisis reveals what an organization and its people are really made of. Sometimes organizations step up and meet the challenge—using their character and values to guide their decision-making. And sometimes organizations fail—they have a weak or inconsistent response. It's my personal belief that, in most cases, these failures can be traced directly to a lack of character or strong values.

Why did so many companies dig so deep to help during the COVID-19 global pandemic, in some cases, taking a painful hit to their bottom lines in the process? Sure, marketing and good customer relations were likely part of the equation for these businesses. But I would like to think that a much greater factor was that the core values of these companies compelled them to make the decisions they made. I'm sure if I asked any of the CEOs of these companies why they did what they did, the response would be "It was simply the right thing to do."

The IBM Work-from-home Pledge

The COVID-19 global pandemic has profoundly changed our world, and it will remain changed for years or perhaps even decades to come. Many companies quickly jumped on the work-from-home bandwagon—encouraging or mandating that employees work in their homes (or wherever they could get a good phone and Wi-Fi connection)—and I expect that, even as the COVID-19 virus runs its course, many employees will continue to work from home instead of returning to the office.

For the companies that quickly shifted from an office-based to a home-based work environment, in many cases, there were no guidelines to ensure everyone knew the new rules of work. That's one of the reasons why I particularly like the Work-from-home Pledge that IBM CEO Arvind Krishna shared with the company's employees in the last week of April 2020. As Krishna points out, it wasn't a top-down mandate. "Created by IBMers," explained Krishna, "this grassroots initiative took shape by listening to colleagues and wanting to help with their challenges, this has evolved into a company-wide pledge with the simple goals of making work (and life) a little easier while we're working at home."[12]

The pledge clearly demonstrates the company's people-first values while providing employees with guidelines for how to behave during these unprecedented times. The emphasis is on enabling flexibility and adaptability while maintaining connection and ensuring that people don't become isolated as they work outside their normal in-house team structures—all with an extra dose of compassion and kindness.

It's a reminder that, in times of crisis, we need to be *human*—we need to ensure that, when it comes to our values, we're walking our talk. Each and every day of the week.

Here's the text of IBM CEO Arvind Krishna's pledge to his employees:

As the CEO of IBM, I pledge to support my fellow IBMers working from home during COVID-19.

I pledge to be Family Sensitive.

I want everyone on a video call with me to know that if they have to put a call on hold to handle a household issue, it is 100 percent OK. No one wants a loved one getting hurt, falling, or breaking something because you were on video.

I pledge to support Flexibility for Personal Needs.

I acknowledge we are all balancing our work and personal lives in new circumstances. I encourage those homeschooling, providing care to others, or addressing other personal needs to block time on their calendar during the day to be able to focus on those activities, as needed. And, I pledge to respect those boundaries when scheduling meetings.

Helpful ask—Please make sure those you work with know that you are away during specified times so they can plan accordingly.

I pledge to support "Not Camera Ready" times.

I will not ask people to turn their cameras on while on video calls. While I encourage the use of video during meetings so we can feel more connected, there will naturally be times when it's just not feasible given home circumstances. During these times, I want everyone to feel comfortable that they can simply turn the video off as needed. Again it's 100 percent OK.

Helpful Ask—Try to have a profile picture so people aren't just staring at your initials. It allows people to "see" you without seeing you.

I pledge to Be Kind.

I will keep in mind that I am "showing up" in others' homes for the first time and want to be a good guest.

I will not make people feel bad about interruptions or make someone feel self-conscious about their surroundings.

As I meet members of my extended work family, I'll roll with it with empathy. It is totally fine if children make noise or jump on camera, or pets make an appearance or say hello—they're family too!

I will show personal interest in a positive way, i.e., if I notice something interesting, I'll ask about its personal significance.

I will not comment on someone's video quality, lighting, background, wall décor (or lack thereof), workspace size, etc.

I pledge to Set Boundaries and Prevent Video Fatigue.

I will use new time limit boundaries for meetings, recognizing video fatigue is real and a new phenomenon for all of us.

I will shift to 20- and 45-minute meetings to replace our normal 30-minute and 1-hour calls as much as possible.

I will avoid setting up any full day or ½ day meetings. If a long meeting is required, I will ensure we take short breaks every hour, that no session is longer than two hours and every two hours there is a 30-minute break.

I pledge to Take Care of Myself.

I will make it a priority to take care of my physical and mental health.

I will stand up frequently, stay hydrated, and try to get the sleep I need.

I will block out time on my calendar to have lunch and dinner AWAY from my workspace.

Where possible I will get outside each day. I'll look for opportunities to change my routine while ensuring social distancing.

I pledge to Frequently Check in on People.

I will frequently check in on the physical and mental health of my coworkers, friends, family, and neighbors, while respecting people's privacy.

I will create space for connection by asking people about their and their loved ones' health & safety in 1:1 settings.

I will send simple text/slack message to just say "Hi, just checking in to see if you and your family are ok" and I'll offer to help if needed (in a genuine way).

I pledge to Be Connected.

I pledge to create social interactions virtually, with my coworkers. Whether it is a coffee break, happy hour, game night or karaoke party, or something else, I will find ways to stay connected.[13]

Cisco and Proposition 8

Much of the brand of a company is based on its behavior and beliefs. Behavior and beliefs that are perceived as positive by customers or the public at large can boost a brand's image and standing, while behavior and beliefs that are perceived as negative can tarnish it. One fact I have discovered over the years is that you cannot create a brand unrelated to how your people act or how you as a company show up every day. Corporate culture, employee behavior, core values, and brand are all tied closely together.

In a 2017 study by Cone Communications, 87 percent of American consumers reported that they would buy a product specifically because the company that produced it advocated for an issue they personally cared about. Conversely, 75 percent of consumers said they would not buy a product if they discovered that the company supported an issue that was against their personal beliefs. Says Alison DaSilva, Managing Director, Purpose & Impact for the Zeno Group communications agency, "Now consumers are no longer just asking, 'What do you stand for?' but also, 'What do you stand up for?'"[14]

The report also revealed that there are five key traits that consumers look for in the companies they choose to do business with:

- Being a good employer;
- Operating in a way that protects and benefits society and the environment;
- Creating products and services that ensure individual well-being;
- Investing in causes in local communities and around the globe; and
- Standing up for important social justice issues.[15]

In 2008, when I was CFO at Cisco, Proposition 8 was listed on the California ballot. The proposition—originally titled the "California Marriage Protection Act"—was an initiative that sought to ban same-sex marriages. At the time, same-sex marriage was a constitutionally protected right in the state of California. Proposition 8 was quite divisive, with the public almost evenly divided for and against. The initiative attracted national attention, with many companies, religious organizations, and individuals vigorously weighing in to either support or defeat it.

I can remember that there was a huge debate and discussion within Cisco's leadership team. Should we come out in support of Prop 8 (which meant banning same-sex marriage) or should we come out against it? Or should we just put our heads down and keep a low profile on the issues, avoiding the controversy altogether? The last outcome any of us wanted was to damage customer relationships or lose business over this initiative.

Sue Bostrom was also at Cisco in 2008, where she served as Executive Vice President and Chief Marketing Officer and Worldwide Head of Government Affairs. Says Bostrom about our internal deliberations:

There was this huge discussion among the leadership team—should Cisco come out and encourage people to vote against Prop 8 and support same-sex marriage? As a company, what do you stand up for and what don't you stand up for? And what do you publicly support or not support? I think these are very important decisions. I was extremely proud that Cisco came out and said, we do not support Prop 8—as a company, we support people being able to marry whoever they love. I think that today, it's important for companies to have good guiding principles. Where are we willing to take a stand?[16]

Despite the very public support that Cisco and other companies offered to those who hoped to defeat Prop 8, the measure passed with 52 percent support, and the California state constitution was amended to include this new provision: "Only marriage between a man and a woman is valid or recognized in California."[17]

Lawsuits were filed, and legal decisions were rendered. The issue of whether Prop 8 was legally enforceable made it all the way to the Supreme Court of the United States, which declined to rule on its constitutionality. This had the effect of killing the measure, returning California to its previous status quo, which considered same-sex marriage to be a right protected by the state constitution. Says Bostrom:

> The decision we made at Cisco at the time was the right one—that everyone has equal rights, equal marriage. We supported this as a company even though some members of our leadership team struggled personally with the idea of gay marriage. As an executive team, there was a lot of debate, and then we came down on the right side of it. Today, there are many topics like this that leaders need to consider, such as, do we require our employees and customers to wear masks to prevent the spread of COVID-19? Many large companies, including Walmart, Home Depot, CVS, Target, and others, now mandate the wearing of masks in their stores. When do we take a stand? Is it different when there is clear science versus politics or beliefs in the mix?[18]

I suggest that, while these may seem like difficult questions on the surface, if we use our core values as our North Star—just as Cisco did more than a decade ago when it decided to come out against Proposition 8—the right thing to do will become crystal clear every time.

The Day the NBA Answered the Call

The National Basketball Association (NBA) is the preeminent basketball league in the world—widely regarded for attracting the very best talent in the sport. The NBA currently comprises 30 teams in the United States and Canada, with total revenue for the league in excess of $8.7 billion a year.[19] Eric Hutcherson is currently the Chief People and Inclusion Officer at Universal Music Group. Before that, he served with the NBA as Executive Vice President and Chief Human Resources Officer. I spoke with Hutcherson to get his perspective on how the NBA showed up when its values were tested.

In 2016, the North Carolina General Assembly passed House Bill 2 (HB2), which was specifically drafted to counter a 7–4 vote of the Charlotte City Council to protect gay and transgender people from discrimination—making them by law a protected class of citizens. One specific part of the Charlotte ordinance that had caught the attention of North Carolina legislators, and the public, was a provision that would allow transgender people to use public restrooms consistent with their self-identified gender.

Just one month after Charlotte passed its antidiscrimination ordinance, the state legislature overrode it by passing HB2, which the governor quickly signed. HB2—nicknamed the "bathroom bill"—quickly gained national attention and condemnation. The bill made it illegal for anyone to use a public bathroom that didn't match the gender on their birth certificate. The bill also barred cities in North Carolina from passing their own ordinances that would be in conflict with HB2.

The ACLU sued the state of North Carolina, asserting in its filing that HB2 was in violation of the Equal Protection Clause of the 14th Amendment to the U.S. Constitution. PayPal announced that it would cancel plans to locate its new global operations center in Charlotte, which would have employed more than 400 people and injected millions of dollars into the local economy. A few days after PayPal's announcement, musical artist Bruce Springsteen cancelled an upcoming concert in North Carolina to protest HB2. Said Springsteen on his website, "Some things are more important than a rock show, and this fight against prejudice and bigotry, which is happening as I write, is one of them."[20]

Eventually, more than 120 companies—including PepsiCo and American Airlines—voiced concerns about HB2 or called for its outright repeal.[21] According to an Associated Press report, North Carolina was projected to lose more than $3.7 billion in foregone business opportunities as a result of HB2.[22]

It was against this backdrop that the NBA was faced with a decision. The basketball league had scheduled its 2017 All-Star Game for February 2017 in Charlotte, home of the Charlotte Hornets, owned by basketball great

Michael Jordan. The NBA had lobbied against HB2, then had to consider its options after the bill was signed into law. Says Hutcherson:

> When HB2 came out in North Carolina, lots of organizations decided that they were not going to do business in the state with that bill in the background. The NBA All-Star Game was scheduled for early 2017, and so we did everything we could to make it be different so we could keep our All-Star Game in North Carolina. But when HB2 was signed by the governor, we realized that we were not going to be able to live to our values, and that having the All-Star Game in Charlotte would be inconsistent with those values. We said we didn't believe that we can put on our showcase event, living to the values that we stand for around equality, and around respect for all, and around equity, to have the bathroom bill in the background. So, at the last minute, we moved the game to New Orleans.[23]

Before making the decision to move the All-Star Game from Charlotte to New Orleans, the NBA had voiced its concerns about HB2 on a number of occasions. These concerns were ultimately ignored by the North Carolina governor and legislature, and the law remained in place. That left the NBA with a choice: It could either set aside its values and keep the All-Star Game in Charlotte, or it could lean into its values and move the game elsewhere. The organization chose to lean into its values and to bear the consequences of its decision.

In a statement regarding its decision, the NBA said, "While we recognize that the NBA cannot choose the law in every city, state, and country in which we do business, we do not believe we can successfully host our All-Star festivities in Charlotte in the climate created by HB2." According to the NBA, the All-Star Game would only be held in a city that could "ensure that all patrons—including members of the LGBT community—feel welcome while attending games and events in their arena."[24]

When the NBA was called, they answered with upstanding character, making the decision to do what was right, not what was most expedient or what offered the greatest contribution to the organization's bottom line. Explains Hutcherson:

> That's an example of corporate character in my mind, in the sense that we had to make a decision as to what we thought was right, and what we thought was wrong. And at that moment, we had to do what needed to be done, even if it was going to have a negative financial impact on the company.[25]

According to Hutcherson, the NBA models what he calls the "new employee value proposition." This new value proposition is based on a firm foundation of living your core values and keeping the focus on the prize. Hutcherson says:

> My premise is that the new employee value proposition is just that—corporate values, being a values-driven organization, being an organization that stands for something, being an organization that makes decisions based on those points of view and those commitments as a company, and quite frankly, that leaders are now measured on how consistent they are in the rhetoric that they put out versus the decisions that they make. My point is that, nowadays, the employee value proposition is not about the prestige of the organization. It's not about the name of the organization. It's not about the financial performance of the organization. Those are all table stakes. Now, engagement, commitment, attraction, employer brand is all based on what you stand for and what you don't stand for, what you speak on and what you don't speak on, and what you do and what you don't do about issues that arise.[26]

Hutcherson explains that now is the time for every organization to put its character to the test—to decide what kind of legacy it will leave for future generations. He continues:

> Now is the moment when you have to determine what your place in history is going to be. It's one of those pivot moments when some organizations are going to take a stand and make a statement for where they are in history, and some aren't. Ten years from now, we'll look back and we'll evaluate which companies stepped forward into the fray, and really participated in the dialogue and in the challenge, and which companies stood back and waited to let others take the lead and take the lumps.

> I believe every organization has to ask, "What are we going to specifically do that is actionable?" They must go beyond just standing on the sidelines saying, "We stand against racism." What specific actions are you prepared to take that will change the conversation and change the dynamic?[27]

I agree with Hutcherson's assessment. As we are confronted with challenges coming from every direction, leaders must consider how history will judge the actions we take—or choose not to take—to address them. Will we step forward and tackle these challenges head-on, making bold action our byline, or will we shrink from them, hoping they go away? I suggest that true character is what shows up in times of crisis, and that organizations with upstanding character will always make the right choice.

CHAPTER 9

Stories from Exemplar Companies—and Leaders

"Learning never exhausts the mind."

—*Leonardo da Vinci*

An organization's upstanding character is a reflection of the people in it.

As I got deeper into what makes corporate culture tick—and thinking about my own experiences at IBM, Cisco, Red Hat, Anaplan, and all the companies we did business with—I stepped back and asked myself, "What really drives company character?"

I started to think about the importance of the character of leaders, and how leaders play a critical and strong role in the culture of an organization—both good and bad. A culture can be tested from time to time due to lackluster business results or other factors, but if you truly have a strong foundation of a good culture, the company is much more likely to withstand the different challenges that may come up.

An organization's upstanding character ultimately derives from the individuals who are a part of the organization—the people who most hold it near and dear to them. This, of course, includes you as a leader, but it also encompasses the people that you surround yourself with—your leadership team, frontline employees, board members, and other stakeholders. What ultimately creates a strong and enduring culture is intentionally nurturing the organization's character.

One of the great benefits about writing this book was it gave me time to talk with others—both inside and outside Anaplan—and get new perspectives. I learned a lot from these discussions, and in this chapter, I'm sharing what I took away from each one. I hope you learn as much from reading these stories as I did.

Adobe: Evolution of a Great Company

Adobe, founded in 1982 by John Warnock and Charles Geschke, is a multinational software company with more than 21,000 employees and over $11 billion in annual revenues. The company is led by Shantanu Narayen, who joined the company in 1998 as Vice President and General Manager of Adobe's engineering technology group, then was named CEO in 2007 and chairman of the board in 2017.

Narayen is widely credited for transforming the company—and the industry—when he pioneered the idea of selling cloud-based subscriptions for Adobe's Creative Suite. I asked him how he thought a leadership change affects the culture of an organization.

> When the core values are serving the organization well, I think core values remain the same. But the culture actually evolves in a company depending upon the needs of the business. Character is really best demonstrated in adversity. People do what you inspect, not what you expect. So, when there is a certain attribute that you want or need—whether you amplify it, whether you recognize it, whether you congratulate it—that plays a much bigger role in a company's culture than what's written on a wall somewhere.

> There's no question in my mind that when you're in an intellectual property business like Adobe it's all about people. When you're in a business where our biggest assets are our people and our employees, how they behave in terms of character, culture, and values is incredibly important. This is especially true of tech companies, more than anywhere else. We all spend more time at work than we probably spend at home. In the greatest companies in the world, individuals perform their best when they resonate with the mission and values and character of a company.

> We're not here just building widgets—we're trying to change the world through digital experiences. My hope is that all our employees feel they

can do their best work and that will be reinforced by the company. Culture has a big influence on this. And, especially as companies scale, that's the bigger challenge. With smaller companies, it's so much easier to get a perspective on what that culture is and how you scale it.

For the last five years at Adobe, I've used the example of the Golden State Warriors basketball team. Anybody can win a championship once, but how do you become a dynasty? What sports teams do better than anybody else, when they're on top, is they have no fear of changing. Golden State made key trades that changed its roster. In sports there's that constant—if you're not practicing, if you're not constantly improving, somebody else is. And so, you're always looking over your shoulder because there's somebody who wants that perch you're on.[1]

I agree 100 percent with Narayen that we can't be complacent. People and organizations must continue to evolve. One of the characteristics of engaged, online character as described by Cy Wakeman is you're never done learning. It's important to constantly raise the bar to improve the success and results of the company.

The pandemic has tested us in new ways, and we've seen people coming together and rising to the challenge whether it's doing business virtually or responding to urgent situations like protests or natural disasters. The times we're in have forced us to be more resilient. The year 2020 was a particularly difficult one for many businesses, but those with upstanding character stood out from the rest. They made a point of providing flexibility, support, and continuity for employees destabilized by the near-constant challenges they faced.

Culture at Puppet—A Move Back to Its Roots

Yvonne Wassenaar is CEO of Puppet—an innovative provider of software solutions that automate how its clients continuously deliver, make compliant, remediate, and manage their multi-cloud environments. Before becoming CEO in 2019, Wassenaar served as CEO of Airware, CIO of New Relic, and Office of the CXO of VMware. In addition, she is currently a member of the board of directors of Anaplan and Forrester, and she is a board trustee at Harvey Mudd College.

I asked Wassenaar to tell me about her own experience with character and culture in the many companies she's worked for and advised, and how that informs what she does today as a CEO.

When you speak about character versus culture, I feel it's a much richer conversation. What does character really mean? I think the character of a company is one part what they do, be it a service or a product. What is the quality in what they make? When I think about Accenture, New Relic, VMware, and Puppet, a meaningful element of how I think about the character of these companies is the high standards of product/offering quality that shows up in the reliability of the offerings and the trust they subsequently have built over many years with their customers. This is a big piece of what company character is all about.

Another part of the character of a company is the culture that it has, who they attract to work there, and in turn, who's servicing you. By that I mean, how does a company show up? Are they fun and playful? Are they stern? Are they boastful? What is their persona and who is it in service to? When I think about New Relic, during its prime we had a great sense of purpose and connection with developers. It was all about developer love. It was so clear who we were engaging with and why, and how we showed up. If you talked about New Relic, you knew it was a bleeding-edge technology company, it was very grassroots—there was a certain feel about it.

As somebody who's come in as CEO to guide a company, you're given a certain set of things. There's the quality of the product. There's the engagement of your employees. There are the values that are espoused. If I take Puppet as an example, I've been here a year and a half and during that time the character of the company has shifted much more back to its roots.

Through a ton of focus on what we did, not just what we said, we improved employee NPS from 2.4 to over 19 in nine months while we were making hard decisions around ending products, letting people go, and shifting the organization. The core that guided us in a positive direction through these hard decisions was purpose. Ultimately, when you take a group of people of good moral standing, and you provide them with a purpose that resonates with them, they can build great technology, they can provide great service, and they can do it in an authentic way that will resonate with people.

In my experience, the leader has the potential to play a tremendous role in developing that purpose and influencing that character. Let me put it this way: I think some leaders let the character evolve around them. But I think companies with great character have leaders who will make hard choices, who will take a stand, who will defend the values that they truly believe and are trying to cultivate.[2]

I was intrigued by Wassenaar's assertion that there are distinctly different parts to a company's character. One part is what they do—a service or product—and the quality and reliability that it embodies. This builds trust. Another part of a company's character is its culture and the people the company attracts.

I also agree that making hard choices and tradeoffs is where company character really comes through. When Cisco faced a significant downturn, we tried every possible avenue to cut costs before laying off employees. These were some of the hardest choices I ever made, but what helped was that people recognized we had to change for the health of the overall business.

We've seen a similar spirit emerge during the pandemic, with managers being extra supportive of their employees who need more flexibility to get through this time. We've tried to lead from a place of always putting people first—when we take care of them, they take care of the business.

All in all, says Wassenaar, leaders play a tremendous role in developing the organization's purpose and influencing its character. Leaders need to be online and have purpose and focus when it comes to managing their company's character—their customers, employees, and other stakeholders can't afford for them to be offline; there's too much at stake in an increasingly competitive and values-focused world.

A Breath of Fresh Air at Coca-Cola

Coca-Cola is an Anaplan customer. I talked with two leaders there, Sara Park and Victor Barnes. Both talked about the company's enduring legacy of community activism as well as how its culture has evolved through a CEO transition.

Sara Park is Vice President, Integrated Planning for The Coca-Cola Company, where she has served for more than eight years. Before that, Park was Director, Supply Chain Planning at Georgia-Pacific.

I asked Park to tell me about how Coca-Cola's culture changed in the transition from the previous Chairman and CEO Muhtar Kent to the current chairman and CEO James Quincey.

Character within Coca-Cola has evolved a lot. When I joined the company, Muhtar Kent was Chairman and CEO. He had been there for a while, but I had never met him in person. He was kind of this mythical person who had an entourage of at least five, six people whenever we saw him on the Coca-Cola campus, which was pretty big. He sat on the highest floor of the global building, which is taller than the USA building. These are all subtle cultural signals, right? He was always in a three-piece suit, even on casual Friday. The impression he projected was authority and tradition, what we would consider now to be kind of the stodgy corporate leadership.

It was a breath of fresh air when James Quincey took over as CEO in 2017. He is in jeans and a button-down shirt, and he wears sneakers. He comes down to the coffee shop by himself, gets in line like everybody else. Sometimes he meets with people in the coffee shop, or he goes and just sits at a table by himself. He's very friendly, and that's the modern image of leadership that he projects. He's very approachable, but at the same time, he's not shying away from setting really ambitious, high goals. He brought in a change mindset—an agile mindset—that became the cornerstone of how our culture should be built. So that's agility, iteration, inclusiveness, and curiosity, and he talks about those values every town hall, every chance he gets. And so, he was slowly but surely starting to change how we come to work.

It took a little while, especially at the SVP and C levels because turnover doesn't happen very often at that level. In the U.S. business, we started to really notice things pretty quickly. We could see how relaxed he is, the way he dresses, he never has an entourage, and this whole change mindset—the agility, the iteration, all of that. There's that saying that you have to say the same thing 50 times for people to really understand. So, every chance he got, he talked about these behaviors, the growth mindset, because that was very, very important for him to change the culture of the company.[3]

I strive to be more like James Quincey, someone who's approachable, empathetic, and able to make a personal connection with employees. The more that people can relate to you as a leader, the easier it is to be a role model for the kind of character you want to see in your organization. This is how personal and company character become intertwined.

Victor Barnes is VP/Global CFO for the McDonald's Division of The Coca-Cola Company, where he has worked for more than 25 years—rising through the company's finance ranks. He previously founded and served as CEO and Coaching Director for the Georgia Stars, a basketball and mentoring organization for youth.

I asked Barnes to tell me about Coca-Cola's corporate culture, how he fits into it, and where he sees it going in the future.

The character of The Coca-Cola Company, I think at its core, is about trying to be a good corporate citizen. That despite the fact that there are key aspects of our culture that need to evolve. We tend to seek perfection over progress, and we therefore end up being too slow and small competitors eat our lunch and innovate in new categories. There are aspects of our culture that are not right, but I think our character generally is in tune with what we want to be. One of the highest-scoring areas on our employee engagement surveys is "being a good corporate citizen," and that's one of the reasons that I have been here over 25 years.

We do have a true north and it's there. The framework of the company is about being an upstanding citizen within the world, and then you're just trying to be part of helping the company perfect that—you can anchor yourself in that belief.

People can totally reject the product; they don't need to be hydrated by Coca-Cola, they can drink water and they will be fine. So how we actually make the brand special is trying to make sure that we stay out in front of the things we know consumers care about. So racial justice— we've got advertising that can be fairly balanced. We support causes like 100 Black Men of America, which is recognized as the nation's top African American-led mentoring organization. We do the right things that give people a sense of our connectivity to community.

But inside our four walls, the truth is that, for my 25 years, we have been primarily a white male-led organization in our flagship market. I'll just focus in the United States for a second. That's just a fact. And the heartbeat of our organization is around driving top-line growth through brand building and innovation and portfolio, and in America—which definitely is increasingly a black and brown country—you don't have leaders in the room who reflect that? You're not necessarily going to have the ideas in the room to provide what consumers want; the people in that room are more likely to overlook potential insights that drive important metrics such as employee experience or brand love. And I would suggest that if we repeat the history of having an organization that's top heavy with white male leadership, we're just asking for a repeat of the last 20 years where competitors have eaten our lunch.

There's a business case for racial justice and diversity, it's not just a social good. It's not just about company character. It's self-preservation, frankly.[4]

Barnes is a change agent in an organization that still resists change, despite the new emphasis on agility brought into Coca-Cola by its current CEO James Quincey. Of course, The Coca-Cola Company has good reason not to change too quickly—in addition to creating great products that people love, it has to protect the value of one of the most visible and well-known brands in the world.

When Barnes questioned why he, as a change agent, was still there—working for a company that was slow to change—he came to the realization that it was because of the company's fundamental character. What he said about being a good corporate citizen really resonates with me. It's one of the reasons I'm active in the Bay Area Council, an organization that brings together business leaders to support civic and community initiatives.

Anaplan is also a big supporter of the Juvenile Diabetes Research Foundation (JDRF) that assists with disease prevention and management and ultimately seeks a cure for type 1 diabetes. This started as a local fundraising effort in one office, and over time, it spread to several offices and is now a global campaign for us. Since 2017, our employees have raised more than $250,000 for this very worthy cause. I've found that when you get people together and have a good time in support of a good cause, it's a wonderful way to build character and support the community at the same time.

Creating a Mission-driven Culture at Chegg

Founded in 2005, Chegg is an education technology company that rents textbooks and provides online tutoring and other educational services. The company—with annual revenues in excess of $410 million—is proud of its values-driven culture, which according to Chegg's website includes "having integrity through transparent, candid, and authentic communication; dreaming big and innovation; and teamwork, constantly adding energy and making others around you better."[5] Dan Rosensweig has served as President and CEO of Chegg since 2010, and before that, he was COO of Yahoo! and president of CNET Networks.

I asked Rosensweig to tell me how he learned what makes good—and bad—character, and how this affected how he built Chegg into a company with character.

I've had the good fortune that almost every boss I've ever worked with had good character, which meant that there was always a balance between the company's productivity and the importance of the human being. Working at Ziff Davis taught me the value of seeing that balance. There were plenty of times where I didn't get what I thought I deserved, but in those moments, my leaders sat me down and had a discussion with me about why, at that time, it was not the right thing for the company or for me. We then had a conversation about my career, how best to develop, and the opportunities for me. That was good leadership character in action.

That investment of their time in me is a great example of the importance of character because they had to make a difficult choice but were willing to show me respect and teach me the way to handle challenging moments that impact people's lives. They sent a clear and positive message to me. So, I learned a lot from having great bosses.

But here's what it meant for Chegg. There was a period when our company was not succeeding. There were several times where the company almost went bankrupt. We were a private company and we needed capital. We had 10 members on our board, and many of the board members had conflicting interests with each other and with the company, depending on when they invested and under what terms. All were understandably concerned about their investment at that time and some focused more on their issues versus those of the others, the company, and our employees. As a result, the board meetings could be toxic at times, making it challenging to make hard decisions and even recruit independent board members. I literally had to beg current board members to give up their seat.

We knew it was important to ensure that our leadership, including our board, was focused on the same issues to give the company a chance to survive and thrive. Having to expend energy on the board, versus operating issues, was exhausting and unhelpful. It took me three years to remove certain board members who were not adding value. While it was hard at the time to bring on new ones, we stayed focused on our goal and ultimately changed the makeup of the board because the character and integrity of that team really mattered.

Companies with character—that can focus on a mission—form a team with a foundation of honesty, transparency, and trust, where the people that assume the best intent are quite often the ones that succeed. When character and integrity are your corporate foundation, you get people discussing the bigger issues of how to provide a better service, build a better company, and support more people, rather than the discussions over how come I'm not paid two percent better than so-and-so, or so-and-so is a problem child, or why aren't you taking my suggestion rather than someone else's suggestion?

Character is built through shared experiences, through trust, through risk-taking with each other, by actually listening to that person and embracing their uniqueness and their differences as voices that will add to the conversation rather than distract from the conversation. But the only way to do that is to hire people with good character.[6]

Rosensweig was fortunate to work for companies early in his career that took the time to explain to him the career path he was on, and why certain decisions were made even when he did not agree with them. There will always be situations when you can't fully align. I recommend a simple phrase to follow: debate, then commit. We need to come together and consider different perspectives (debate), but then once a decision is made, we need to follow through, move forward, and make it successful (commit).

I also think it's critical that leaders be candid with their employees—people want to know the truth, even if it hurts. Telling the truth in a direct and constructive way builds trust, and trust is the foundation that strengthens and supports all relationships.

The Nature of Character at Slack

The business communication platform developed by Slack Technologies has quickly become ubiquitous, one of a handful of companies whose name has become a verb: "Can you Slack it to me?" Allan Leinwand is the Senior Vice President of Engineering for Slack, and he previously served as CTO for ServiceNow. Before that, he worked for Zynga, Panorama Capital, Cisco, and HP. He is on the Anaplan board of directors and is a member of the Forbes Technology Council.

I asked Leinwand to tell me about how character is expressed at Slack and how this character affects the company's relationships with customers, partners, and employees.

> I think the character of a company is defined by the interaction between the company, its customers, and its partners. How the character of the company is expressed needs to be driven almost top down at times. I've worked at a few different companies, and sometimes you see CEOs and senior leaders exemplify the behavior they want to see in the company. For example: we're not going to be an aggressive sales team—we're going to be a partnership sort of company. And there are other companies that I've worked with where they have the opposite approach: we're going to be an aggressive sales team and we're going to go after the numbers. It's interesting to study and assess what works, or doesn't, and why.

> I find that the character of the company is driven by senior leadership and how they want that company to be viewed in the world. I think about some of the meetings I've had at Slack or ServiceNow, where we have these discussions about how do we want to treat our employees? How do we want to treat our partners? How do we want to treat our customers?

> Character is really important to us at Slack. It's a company that is both focused on building a collaboration product and focused on the customer. We're also very empathetic to what our customers are trying to do. We listen carefully to our customers and try and produce products that meet their needs. We're also empathetic internally in terms of listening to our employees and trying to make sure that they embody what we do.

At Slack, we have four characteristics we talk about: smart, humble, hardworking, and collaborative. By smart, we don't mean intelligence—it's doing the right thing at the right time for the customer. Hardworking is the "work hard, play hard" thing, but in a Slack perspective, we want to make sure people get the right work done at the right time. Humble is super important for our character because we don't think of ourselves as this company that's going to dominate the world. Certain companies come out and say, "We will dominate!" We don't have that ethos around us. And collaborative because we build collaboration products and we want to make sure that people work together on a shared outcome. Those are the attributes that we try and hire for, that we try and emulate, and that we want our character to demonstrate to our customers.[7]

In Leinwand's experience, a company's character is driven by its senior leadership team and how they want the company to be viewed in the world. I like how "humble" is one of the four characteristics. Similar to what Sara Park said, being overly formal or dictatorial isn't the best way to gain respect and loyalty. Instead, I think leaders who are humble and approachable—you might say *authentic*—are better at connecting with people and building relationships that contribute to lasting success. Being humble means recognizing there are people smarter than you, and always being open to learning and hearing different points of view.

In my own experience, the CEO and executive leadership team set the pace for a company's culture. While culture is the sum of how every employee shows up, the direction is set by the senior leadership team. Allan's description of the values guiding Slack and their commitment to their people and their customers I thought was a great example of a company character aligned to all the factors that make upstanding character urgently relevant now.

Charles Schwab: A Founder's Living Legacy of Service to Clients

Elizabeth King is Senior Vice President, Enterprise Learning and Talent Management for Charles Schwab, where she has served for three years, and before that, she was Vice President, HR Worldwide Sales at Cisco. Charles Schwab Corporation—founded by its namesake and Chairman Charles

Schwab in 1971—pioneered the discount stock brokerage model and is today the third-largest asset manager in the world, with more than $4.5 trillion in client assets.

I asked King to describe how having the company's founder and namesake still actively involved in the company has affected its culture.

When I had been at Schwab for about nine months I was asked to do some executive assessments for some very senior folks, for the board. And so, I had an opportunity to interview five board members, as well as probably 16 EVPs, and some SVPs for these assessments.

And, so it was a chance to learn a lot about those people, but also about the environment in which they operate. I remember very distinctly some of the conversations I had with the board, and there's a subset of the Schwab board that has been with Chuck for decades. They were talking about Schwab being purpose-driven, and the service to people in the financial space, and helping people achieve fundamental financial goals such as buying a house, sending their kids to college, saving for retirement, and serving philanthropic needs and legacies for families.

It became clear to me in that moment that, for some of these people, this is almost spiritual. They feel a calling to do this for as many people as they can—not just wealthy people, but for as many people as possible. They feel that providing access to the markets and helping people plan and save and achieve those kinds of goals is their purpose—why they're there. It comes straight from Chuck, and you could feel it in the place because that's what he believes.

You feel this intensity from people on the board and all the leaders. They get choked up sometimes; they feel so strongly about this passion. I like that. It's a for-profit company, but you can feel that core character. In addition to grit and perseverance and a number of other great character traits that you see in Chuck, you see this deep commitment to the service of people that's just threaded through the place.

Success at Schwab requires a profile that is in service of others. And so, you have a profile that's not overambitious, that's more humble, understated, team oriented, and collaborative. All those things line up so that you are in service to clients.[8]

Charles Schwab has a culture of service to its clients—some of Schwab's board members have been with the company for decades, which provides an unprecedented level of continuity. It's a calling for these people, just as it is for founder Charles Schwab. Organizations that have been around a long time have a strong purpose and it resonates. People enjoy being there and they have lasting careers. Schwab is laser-focused on its purpose, which is to help people achieve their fundamental financial goals, and it goes way beyond Chuck—it really cascades throughout the organization.

Genpact: Character Drives Client-first Culture

Tiger Tyagarajan is President and CEO of Genpact, where he has worked for more than 15 years, and a board member of Catalyst Inc. Genpact is a global professional services firm that works with Global Fortune 500 companies to solve complex problems and accelerate digital transformation using data and analytics. The company reported annual revenues of $3.52 billion in 2019.

I asked Tyagarajan to tell me how culture has evolved over the years in his company and how it is keeping up with emerging trends in the workforce.

I have always been a big believer that the most important thing that determines long-term, sustainable success and value creation for employees, for clients, and for the business is the character of the company. I don't use the word "character" that much—I use the word "culture" a lot, but I think it's similar. So, what is the culture of the company? What is the culture of the people?

Clients love working with us because we all see a true north as a team, and irrespective of where they touch the company and who they interact with, they get the same reaction and they feel the same culture. That culture for us boils down to "the only thing that matters is the client."

At various points in time, we've hired people based on culture and we've let people go based on culture. And we evaluate people on two dimensions—performance on one axis and culture and values on the second axis. And the toughest conversation we have is with someone who is high on performance but low on values and culture because that's the person to whom you need to say, "What do you want to do?"[9]

Tyagarajan makes a great point here, and this is one of the hardest things any leadership team will face—what to do about a high performer who is not aligned in terms of values and character. What I've seen is that, if you don't address toxic behavior—rudeness, arrogance, bullying, and the like—it becomes a cancer in the organization. Sometimes other people will copy the behavior, sometimes great people will leave because they can no longer put up with the bad behavior—there is quite literally a cost to keeping badly behaving people around.

Cy Wakeman describes what she calls "emotionally expensive" employees—those who may be successful by conventional metrics but create drama and drain the energy of the people around them. In the long run, they are not worth it.[10]

Tyagarajan also had this to say about how to manage differences of opinion:

One of the things we value in our culture is debate. If you attend one of my leadership team meetings of 15 people on a topic, such as how do we add value in the supply chain for our clients, that conversation may go on for two hours because there can be five different opinions that are debated. And when I say "debate," it's an aggressive debate—people are duking it out. But there's a lot of trust—the debate is professional, not personal. At the end of that evening, we say, "Ok, now let's go for a drink," and we celebrate the fact that I had a great debate and we've got a good answer.

Debate like this really works only if you have different opinions in the room and people are willing to fight for them. You have people with different perspectives—"The sun is going to rise in the west—let me prove it to you." How do you include people who have those different opinions, and then foster a culture where people have the courage to actually speak their mind on various topics, even though they realize that 10 of the people in the room have an opposite view? As a leader, you've got to foster that. If you foster that, then you get different opinions. If you get different opinions, you are able to shape better answers and better solutions. So, we've been on this journey of bringing people with different opinions into the room and creating a culture of inclusion. And that includes people with different global backgrounds, gender—all kinds of diversity.

I'm a big believer that if you want to drive a certain culture, if you want to drive diversity and inclusion, as an example, you have to find a way to connect it to business. Because if you don't, then it loses steam. Just telling people it's the right thing to do, and it's a good thing to do, only gets you so far because the pressure of business gets to you. You've got to find a way to make sure that it makes sense for the business and then make sure it's connected.[11]

I like Tyagarajan's focus on a culture of debate, where diverse ideas are encouraged, put on the table, and then aggressively fought over in a civil, but forceful way. It's clear that ideas aren't greenlighted just because someone high up in the hierarchy suggested it. Regardless of who suggested them, these ideas must be strong enough to survive the debate before they'll see the light of day. And as I mentioned before, once the debate is over and a decision is made, everyone commits to supporting the decision moving forward.

Ultimately, a company's culture must connect to the business in some tangible way, and Tyagarajan makes sure in Genpact's case that it does.

Keeping the Culture Ball in Play at Splunk

Splunk—founded in 2003—makes software used for searching, monitoring, and analyzing machine-generated big data. The company, which has annual revenues of more than $2 billion, is run by CEO Doug Merritt, who has served at Splunk for more than six years. Before taking the reins as CEO in 2015, Merritt was Senior Vice President Field Operations for the company. Before Splunk, he was Senior Vice President Product and Solution Marketing at Cisco, and Corporate Officer at SAP as well as President of SAP Labs.

I asked Merritt to tell me how Splunk's company character has come into play during this particularly challenging year, and how he keeps everyone aligned with the company's core values and culture.

Splunk's culture has been incredibly important to help us through the challenges of 2020. One of my favorite Splunk mantras is that it's "always the right thing, to do the right thing." As a social species, we innately understand that supporting each other is key to our mutual success. At Splunk, we want to be inclusive, we want to be empathetic and take the other perspective into consideration. Our core values and beliefs as a company help provide the benefit of the doubt. With over 6,000

Splunkers, there are bound to be instances of non-alignment across the company. It's unrealistic to expect to be uniform and totally aligned with that many people, but we keep leaning on our core values, our company priorities, and our leadership principles. The clarity that these provide are key to help make sure that we are doing the right thing for the collective whole.

What's been really interesting for me to watch over the past five years, and then really accelerated over the past few months, is extremist behavior and how the middle ground is not very well thought of right now. There's been so much written about social media and the filters that are feeding groups of people more and more information that reaffirms that their position is absolutely and undeniably right. This results in so much energy away from the middle and to the edges.

How I've watched this show up inside of companies is through a shift away from a "disagree and commit" culture. One of the strong benefits of a democracy is the right for anyone and everyone to speak—to be heard. However, after everyone is heard, a decision still needs to be made. Right now, if you've got 3 percent, 4 percent that disagree—and you always will, it's a natural bell curve—that 3 percent, 4 percent will not be happy with a decision that isn't the decision they wanted. It's not, "I want you to listen to me, I want a fair environment to be heard," it's "I want you to listen to me and you must change your beliefs and your behaviors to conform to mine."

That's not what diversity or democracy is about. The point of diversity is to bring 10, 20, or 500 groups with different opinions together, and getting to really benefit from that divergence in thinking and opinion. But then again, you eventually have to make a decision. And the nature of the decision means that, if you have a hundred people in a room, all hundred can't be happy. It's not a decision if all hundred people are happy.

I hate to be repetitive, but ultimately, I think we are dealing with the barbells of scarcity versus abundance. Of fear versus love. We all have the freedom to adopt our own belief systems. Clarity on beliefs helps with consistent decision making. Consistency in decision making defines character. When beliefs, decisions, and actions are aligned, there is a clear and defined character.

I think these coming years are going to be a new level of tests on our beliefs . . . and our character. I've been faced with so many decisions in life that ultimately come back to fear versus love, scarcity versus abundance. The decisions that have worked out the best are those driven by love and abundance. A great example was pivoting Splunk into four-plus simultaneous transformations. That level of change should kill any company. And fear and scarcity thinking was screaming, "Why are you changing a good thing? We're growing. Don't screw it up." But the belief that there was so much more out there for Splunk, and the only way we'd be able to capture that opportunity was to leave what was safe and known, and move to the abundant and expansive unknown.

You know that the risk is off the charts, and a big chunk of the world is going to be able to easily throw darts at your decisions. But it's important to keep that alignment—you can't espouse one thing and do something else. You have to take those actions to continue to drive your character forward.[12]

Like Merritt, I too am concerned that so much behavior in the world around us is being pushed to the extremes at the expense of the middle ground. It's important for businesses to take a stand that is consistent with their character, culture, and values, and sometimes they have to draw the line.

When we conducted values workshops to solicit input on the new Anaplan values, we were very collaborative and involved everyone in the process, but we did not achieve 100 percent agreement—and that's OK. Not everyone agreed with every word we picked, but they appreciated the opportunity to contribute and have their ideas listened to.

The Power of Jaguar Land Rover's Mantra

Jaguar Land Rover (JLR) of Whitley, Coventry, United Kingdom, traces its origins to 1922 and the Swallow Sidecar Company. The first Jaguar automobile was built in 1935 and the company's sports cars pushed the limits of speed—and technology—for decades. The Land Rover utility 4x4 vehicle was introduced in 1948, and it quickly became the standard for rugged, off-road expeditions and for providing life-saving relief to people in disasters and war. The combined brand is today a part of India's largest automotive manufacturer, Tata.

I talked with Mike Tickle, who is Planning Director, Commercial at Jaguar Land Rover, about the Commercial team's unique approach to enshrining its team character.

We have created a mantra that I think is very much a personification of what might be described as company character. We drew a star and put our "Customer First" ethos in the center of it. The star has five points, and each point represents a different value: Positively Passionate, Relentlessly Driven, Creatively Bold, Agile Entrepreneurs, and Consummate Professionals. And when we talk about the strategies and the mantra within our team, the strategies represent what we need to get out and do, and the mantra is about how we show up to do it. In my understanding, our mantra is a fair representation of a company's character, and I've seen some of our senior leaders really embrace it.

There are always people that want to be negative in most any organization. However, it's those who are positively passionate that we find are the can-do people that have really driven us forward. They make sure everybody is recognized for the delivery they've achieved, even if we might have always sold one unit more. We achieve a lot along the way because of the journey we're going through together.

I've seen peers of mine be really positively passionate about that aspect, for example. They lift the team as they do that. When everyone around you is saying, "Yeah, but you're not good enough" and "It's still not enough," it's the positively passionate people who create that safety space for everyone to drive forward. If you listen too much to the negativity—"Yeah—it's not good enough"—then it can have a really negative impact on the team.

We designed the mantra as a leadership team, and we've cascaded it to the whole of our global commercial team, 3,000 employees around the world. And we've asked everybody to embrace both the what—the strategy—and the how, which is how we want people to turn up, the commercial mantra. We absolutely said it can't be leadership only. It needs to be leadership team-led, but it absolutely has to cascade and permeate throughout the organization. Everybody has to bring it to life. And it ensures we stay focused on our overall purpose at Jaguar Land Rover: delivering Experiences People Love, For Life.[13]

I really like the idea of having a corporate mantra—a set of values that drives employee behavior. I also like the fact that JLR put its customers at the center of its focus. Ultimately, it's customers who provide the funds that enable a business to exist, scale, and grow.

As Tickle reminds us, it's better to surround ourselves with positive people and to be positive people ourselves—*positively passionate*. A real can-do attitude to get stuff done.

CHAPTER 10

Looking to the Future

"What you do makes a difference, and you have to decide what kind of difference you want to make."

—Jane Goodall

Create the future you want to live and work in.

It's an interesting exercise to imagine what our workplaces will look like sometime in the future—a year, a decade, a generation.

I see organizations that have overcome the biases and structural issues that we currently struggle with, that are more equitable and more inclusive than they are today. I mean *profoundly* more equitable, *profoundly* more inclusive.

I see organizations that encourage and reward employees for engaging in constructive debate—to fight hard over *ideas* and not *personalities*.

I see organizations that are boundary-less—with teams that function just as well with people physically in the office as with people who are distributed and working remotely, anywhere, anytime.

I see organizations that use technology to unleash the creativity, power, and passion within every employee, and that enable us to stay connected to each other in ways that are liberating, not confining.

If there's a time when we need to make sure every employee has a seat at the table, is included in the conversation, and feels a deep sense of belonging to their team and their company, that time is *now*.

If there's a time when we need to change the way we lead our people and our organizations, that time is *now*.

In this final chapter, I explore how we can do just that.

The AI Edge

The Black Lives Matter movement reminds every CEO, including myself, that we must never lose our focus on improving the diversity and inclusiveness of our workforces. We have to do this in a way that actually makes a long-term, systemic change to how we recruit and retain talent. Unfortunately, despite our best efforts, the numbers just aren't there yet—especially in the technology sector.

The advantages of a diverse workforce have been well researched and proven. According to McKinsey & Company, "Diverse teams are more innovative—stronger at anticipating shifts in consumer needs and consumption patterns that make new products and services possible, potentially generating a competitive edge."[1] Building a diverse workforce isn't just the right thing to do; it makes good business sense.

And, of course, when we have a diverse group of people in place, we've got to include everyone in the discussion—we have to listen to what all participants have to say. Clearly our efforts aren't good enough—yet. We're making progress overall, but our progress is slower than it should be. Inclusivity is central to upstanding character. Talent isn't limited to just one gender identity or expression, or to any particular religion, race, ethnicity, age, disability status, citizenship, or any other characteristic that makes people unique. We must do better at recruiting and retaining diverse people. Period.

At the end of 2019—before the COVID-19 global pandemic threw millions of people out of their jobs and shuttered thousands of businesses—an estimated 918,000 information technology jobs were left unfilled.[2] As COVID-19 runs its course, and as world economies inevitably rebound, the tech industry will again be in a situation where we'll have hundreds of thousands of unfilled jobs, and finding qualified candidates to fill those jobs will be our focus.

Where will these new hires come from? Where will we find the diverse group of people we need to thrive in the coming years? Correlation One, which is discussed in Chapter 7, is one effort to address this. But we will need multiple approaches to attract a diverse workforce and nurture a workplace culture that ensures everyone is able to bring their authentic selves and contribute their best. But having the right intentions is not enough without concrete actions to ensure inclusivity—both in individual behaviors as well as in programs and systems that support our operations.

To that end, I've been following with great interest a variety of initiatives to apply AI—artificial intelligence—to identifying employment opportunities for people from disadvantaged communities. Not only do these initiatives have implications for creating a workforce that better reflects the communities in which we do business, but they will also help to close the ongoing tech industry hiring gap.

IBM SkillsBuild is one such initiative. SkillsBuild is a "digital platform that provides job seekers—including those with long-term unemployment, refugees, asylum seekers, veterans, and students—with career-fit assessments, training, personalized coaching, and the experiential learning they need to enter or re-enter the workforce."[3] Studies show that the traditional résumé-review process puts women and minorities at a tremendous disadvantage—some estimates say from 50 to 67 percent.[4] For example, when the same résumé is submitted using a "white"-sounding name versus an ethnic-sounding name, the white-sounding applicant gets significantly more callbacks.[5] The application of AI has the potential to solve this problem.

One of the key components of SkillsBuild is a non-biased, AI-based MyInnerGenius Career Fit assessment created by Los Angeles–based GreatBizTools that helps people "discover what they do best with careers that match their natural skills, abilities, and personality—regardless of education or background."[6] Says GreatBizTools President Denise Leaser, the company's AI-based tools take "a full assessment of the individual's cognitive abilities, and creates a comprehensive competency profile that's unique to them, then uses algorithms that match them to jobs that require different competencies."[7] It's expected that these applicants—many of whom have no previous experience in technology, and don't have college degrees—will be trained to fill roles in web development, customer service, and cybersecurity.

Workforce data company Catalyte is also using AI to find diverse job candidates in places where most tech companies aren't currently looking. Catalyte works from the assumption that talented, high-performing job candidates can be found virtually anywhere—they just need the proper training and opportunity. Says CEO Jacob Hsu:

> We're literally hiring truck drivers and teachers, retail workers and fast-food workers...and very rapidly, within 20 weeks, getting them through a computer science degree and getting them into not just actual jobs but proving they can be highest performers in those roles.[8]

These success stories give me hope. While we have a long way to go, I'm convinced that as we continue to shine a spotlight on our shortcomings as an industry, and we continue to apply AI and other leading-edge technology in innovative new ways, we'll be able to create a tech workforce that is more diverse and more inclusive than ever before. The talent is out there, but it's in places where we haven't traditionally been looking. It's in everyone's interest—our customers, our employees, our shareholders, and other stakeholders—that we find talented people wherever they may be and give them the skills and the support they need to succeed.

Career Management

I believe that, in the future, people will pay much more attention to the core values and culture of the companies they choose to work for. I also think that companies will similarly put a much greater emphasis on hiring people who are aligned with their core values and culture. In the former case, we already know that early career employees entering the workforce are pushing back against the rigid constraints of outdated company cultures that value hierarchy over outcomes. According to a recent *New York Times* article, "More of them expect and demand flexibility—paid leave for a new baby, say, and generous vacation time, along with daily things, like the ability to work remotely, come in late or leave early, or make time for exercise or meditation."[9]

While I'm not saying that every company needs to set up meditation rooms or hire personal trainers for its employees, I am saying that every company needs to make its upstanding character clear to the outside world—attracting the kind of people who desire those values and that culture and who will be aligned with them as fully contributing members of the team. And once those people are on board, the company needs to embody and reinforce those values consistently.

When I interviewed Sue Bostrom for this book, she reminded me about an inspiring story that Duke Blue Devils Coach K once told to us at Cisco. Recalls Bostrom:

Coach K shared that he had to take two different buses to get to high school in Chicago. His mom worked two jobs as a cleaning person and was usually just returning home from work as he was getting ready to leave for school. Coach K's mom would tell him, "Make sure you get on the right bus." According to Coach K, this reminder wasn't about getting on the right physical bus. It was more along the lines of saying, "Make sure you hang out with the right people and do the right things today."

I use that story now when I talk to folks about making a decision about a job, or even joining the board of a company—that brand and its values are going to be on your résumé forever. Getting back to the character of a company, I think—especially for this younger generation of workers—the idea about what bus they're getting on, and how they will be affiliated with that bus, is critically important. That's why you see outrage among employees at some companies right now. They got on a bus thinking it represented certain values that they agreed with. And now it's proven to be different and they don't feel as comfortable. They've discovered they're riding on the wrong bus.

It's incumbent upon us to choose leaders, teams, and companies that align with our own personal and professional core values and ethics. Study after study shows that people want to work at companies that share their values. According to a Workplace Culture Trends report published by LinkedIn, "71 percent of professionals say they would be willing to take a pay cut to work for a company that has a mission they believe in and shared values."[10] Says Nina McQueen, Vice President, Global Talent—Benefits, Mobility & Employee Experience at LinkedIn, "While earning potential is always going to be an important aspect of a job, the company's culture is what motivates and inspires workers on a daily basis."[11]

In addition, 70 percent of the professionals in the survey said they would not work at a leading company if it had a bad workplace culture, and 39 percent—almost 2 in 5—said that they would quit their current job "if their employer were to ask them to do something they have an ethical or moral conflict with."[12]

Think about this for a moment. The vast majority of people surveyed want to build their careers with organizations that have a mission they believe in, that share the same values, and that have a good workplace culture. And the same is true for all of us. We all want to build careers with organizations that have missions we believe in, that share the same values we do, and that embody upstanding character.

As we manage our own careers, it's up to us to get on the right bus—to choose leaders, teams, and companies that are aligned with our own personal and professional values and ethics. And when we do, the benefits are many. We've all seen the abysmal engagement statistics regularly published by Gallup (at the time of this writing, the percentage of U.S. employees who are either not engaged or actively disengaged stands at 60 percent).[13] However, while this number is one that every leader should be concerned about, we must keep in mind that some companies have much higher levels of engagement than do others. According to Gallup, organizations with the highest levels of employee engagement have high-development cultures:

> Gallup has studied hundreds of organizations during the past two decades. Many of these organizations have improved substantially over time—some going from less than 20 percent engagement to over 70 percent. These organizations have focused on creating high-development cultures, where people can see their impact on the organization and its customers through their work. They have opportunities to develop their strengths and purpose into a career. This is essential, since the top reason that employees change jobs is to pursue career growth opportunities.[14]

Gallup identified four specific themes that organizations with high-development cultures all share in common:

- **High-development cultures are CEO- and board-initiated.** These organizations have a well-defined purpose and brand, and leaders make engagement relevant to the everyday work of their employees. Top executives initiate the effort, they live it, and they set the course for improvement.
- **High-development cultures educate managers on new ways of managing—moving from a culture of "boss" to "coach."** These organizations have leaders who encourage teams to solve problems themselves instead of issuing top-down commands. Engagement, performance, and training are aligned, and training is tailored to the capacity of leaders.
- **High-development cultures practice company-wide communication.** These organizations have a "champion's network" to communicate best practice examples and stories collected from across the company.
- **High-development cultures hold managers accountable.** These organizations show what they value by recognizing the performance of outstanding team members, while refusing to tolerate mediocrity. In addition, they create high-value career paths for individual contributors

who are not managers, and they "know there is no meaningful mission or purpose in the absence of clear expectations, ongoing conversations, and accountability."[15]

While organizations come with their own values and culture, we don't have to passively accept them. We can either work from within to improve them and make them better and more relevant to current and future workplace trends or we can find an organization that is better aligned with our own values and culture. Authenticity is a tenet of upstanding character. The work of upstanding character is to figure out what you will do to manage values gaps, because it's in the gaps where inauthenticity can lurk—where actions that don't line up to stated intentions can derail organizations. Effectively developing your career, especially as you increase your levels of responsibility and accountability, depends on actively monitoring the potential for gaps in character or values alignment.

The Future of Work

The world is changing faster than ever, and the workplace will change too— for better or worse, depending on how we respond. I personally believe that we can ensure that our organizations change for the better by keeping the North Star of our upstanding character always in sight. I am convinced that success will come to those companies that are agile, resilient, and upstanding—through both good times and bad. As business advisor and entrepreneur Barry O'Reilly explains, "What impacts our business more than anything else is how we respond to unforeseen events."[16]

We got to see this for ourselves with the COVID-19 pandemic, the economic disruption that followed, and the social movements that emerged. However, O'Reilly points out that events such as these don't have to be disruptions. He argues that the pandemic is not a disruption—it's actually an accelerant that is amplifying the advantages of digital businesses that have tremendous insight into consumer habits and the ability to pivot quickly in response to unexpected events. These companies have systems and platforms designed to:

- Gather vast amounts of data;
- Hypothesize and simulate potential scenarios;
- Run small experiments to see if their hypotheses are correct; and
- Iterate to success.

But that's not enough—companies must have the right values to be resilient in the face of these changes. For example, Zoom is a company that exploded in popularity during the pandemic, experienced significant issues (security flaws), but committed to fixing them quickly and transparently. Says O'Reilly, "In a crisis, it can seem like the hardest time to lean into and live your values, but it's also the most important time to do so."[17]

Emerging from the extreme turbulence of 2020, we must take this opportunity to look ahead and address longtime workplace dissatisfiers. Says Marilyn Miller:

> There are lots of things that people were very unhappy with about the way we shaped work prior to COVID-19. If we come out of this and we try to reinstate exactly what we had before, and not solve the deep dissatisfiers around a work-life blend, commuting time, and office space, then shame on us. There are so many things that we can rethink and do better to make work more satisfying for our people.[18]

Rather than seeking a return to the status quo, we have the chance to experiment with something bold and new. The position/agenda/activism framework, introduced in Chapter 7, provides a way to define and navigate what your teams can do on important social issues. We now have the opportunity to reset our organizations, using our character as the prism to guide what we do and how we do it.

I suggest we take the opportunity and run with it.

In fact, there's a movement already formed to redefine access to future-ready careers by rethinking prerequisite qualifications and training. Dave Ricks, CEO of Eli Lilly, and I were talking about a nonprofit startup his company, along with 35 other prominent leading businesses, is backing. OneTen is "an organization that will combine the power of these committed American companies to upskill, hire, and promote one million Black Americans over the next 10 years into family-sustaining jobs with opportunities for advancement."[19] The OneTen launch press release explains:

> OneTen is not just philanthropy. Rather it is a coalition of leaders across industries who are committed to ensuring that Black Americans with the skills and aptitude to earn success also have the opportunity to achieve success. Recognizing that the current system is not inclusive enough and has reinforced systemic barriers that have prevented many Black Americans from the opportunity to earn success, OneTen has set out to change the way companies provide more equitable environments to

drive better business outcomes and benefit all employees. The newly established organization will cultivate an ecosystem that brings together major employers, in partnership with the nation's leading non-profits and other skill-credentialing organizations, to create a more flexible talent pipeline and practices that will allow employees and employers to thrive by shifting to a skills-first paradigm.[20]

According to the *Wall Street Journal (WSJ)*, OneTen has already raised more than $100 million in seed funding. The *WSJ* reports:

> Merck CEO Ken Frazier, one of the startup's founders, said the nonprofit organization will focus on helping Black Americans without four-year college degrees, but with high school diplomas and other certifications, find and retain "family-sustaining jobs," or those earning $40,000 or more depending on the region.[21]

These executives are mobilizing innovation in support of resetting norms, practices, and policies that have long contributed to systemic bias and racism—or just made it too hard for too many to get into and grow a career. It took too long to get here, but this initiative promises to recast the landscape of career opportunity within the foreseeable future. I find the speed and commitment of these leaders stepping up to materially increase access to opportunity incredibly inspiring and encouraging.

Equity-fluent Leadership

For our organizations to thrive both today and in the years to come, we need a new kind of leader. The modern leader of today no longer seeks an unattainable "balance" between work and home; rather, they embrace a work-life blend that favors a healthy integration between the two. They embrace values and a workplace culture that allow more flexibility and autonomy for everyone, while setting the bar high on performance.

Regardless of what kind of business environment we may find ourselves in—whether it's crisis, a downturn, or that sweet spot where everything is going our way—our continued growth and profitability depend on attracting the very best people, including them in everything we do, and creating a sense of belonging that increases their ownership, engagement, and loyalty.

Kellie McElhaney is the Founding Director of the Center for Equity, Gender, and Leadership (EGAL) and a Distinguished Teaching Fellow at the Haas School of Business at University of California, Berkeley. She and her associates have been exploring the idea of something they call equity-fluent leadership.

According to Professor McElhaney, equity-fluent leaders "understand the value of different lived experiences and courageously use their power to address barriers, increase access, and drive change for positive impact." This style of leadership seeks to unlock the creative potential and performance of every employee—not just those in dominant groups. I asked her why equity-fluent leadership is a requirement for businesses to thrive—both today and in the future—and why organizations should give serious consideration to adopting it.

Company leaders are about to manage the most multicultural generation ever in our history as a nation. In my classroom, I ask students how they identify themselves—what their lived identities are. While one identity—straight white female—naturally comes up for me, my undergrad students consistently list five or more distinct identities. They naturally have many more lived identities than most of us in older generations do. And so, from a positive perspective, effectively managing a workforce that is much more diverse than it was in the past is going to require a significant amount of equity fluency from us as leaders.

Unfortunately, there are some significant obstacles in the way. There's a complete and utter lack of courage among leaders to be bold and to speak out against the focus on short-term results and Wall Street's constant pressure on financial returns. There is not enough diversity in leadership. There's a pervasive archetype of good leaders as mostly white and mostly male, as opposed to someone who doesn't fit that archetype physically, or because of their identity, or even just their style. And there aren't enough leaders who have been trained to be equity fluent. One of my alums did a podcast yesterday and he sent it to me—he's in the finance industry. And he said, "I think equity-fluent leadership should be in every business school and in every textbook." My hope is that more leaders will become aware of equity-fluent leadership and get trained in it.

The research clearly shows that diverse teams outproduce teams that aren't diverse, and diverse teams perform tasks with a higher level of collective intelligence. In addition, creativity is higher in companies with diverse teams, and they launch more new products and services. To really isolate it, the costs for messing up on not being equity fluent are swift and significant, particularly for organizations that trend toward being dominated by straight white males. So that's the negative side of it, though I personally prefer to focus on the positives, which are many.[22]

EGAL has created a series of playbooks targeted to different equity issues, including at the time of this writing:

- Supporting dual career couples;
- Mitigating bias in artificial intelligence; and
- Transforming business beyond COVID-19.[23]

The COVID-19 global pandemic created added work for employees who have school-age children at home. With most schools closed until infection rates drop below a specified number for a period of time, many working parents had to juggle the roles of caregiver and home-school teacher—all while trying to maintain their jobs and careers. In most cases, the burden falls disproportionately on mothers, the primary caregivers in many dual-career households. As EGAL points out, "Women in senior leadership positions who have male partners are five times more likely than their partners to do all or most of the household work." In addition, "women experience higher levels of work family conflict than men" and "are twice as likely as men to limit their work commitments."[24]

And the trend toward dual-career couples is on the upswing. While the majority (62 percent) of American full-time employees have a spouse or partner who also works full time, 78 percent of dual-career couples are Millennials versus just 47 percent of Baby Boomers.[25]

The EGAL playbook for supporting dual-career couples outlines seven evidence-based "plays" that any organization can adopt to create a more equity-fluent workplace, while enhancing the performance, satisfaction, and well-being of employees.

Policy and Benefits Plays

- Enable flexible work options.
- Offer and encourage paid parental leave and leave for caretaking.
- Support access to affordable, quality childcare and eldercare.

Mindset, Culture, and Strategy Plays

- Train managers on why and how to support dual-career couples.
- Educate senior leaders about contemporary talent and how to attract/ nurture it; conduct reverse or reciprocal mentoring.
- Develop an employee resource group (ERG) and provide platforms for employees to discuss challenges, and share tips and tools.
- Reevaluate what a successful, ambitious career path looks like and develop geographically flexible options.[26]

Each playbook explains these approaches in great detail, with step-by-step recommendations for putting each play into action, including assigning ownership of the process, identifying what success looks like, gaining internal support, options and alternatives to consider, and evaluating specific business benefits from implementing the play. The playbooks also include case studies of companies that have applied the principles of equity-fluent leadership and have gained positive outcomes.

For example, in response to the COVID-19 global pandemic, Charter Communications gave each of its frontline field technicians and customer service call center workers a permanent raise of $1.50 an hour. The company's goal is for every Charter employee to be paid a minimum of $20 an hour, which is $5 an hour more than the industry norm.[27]

Patagonia provides in-house childcare to more than 250 children of employees at its Ventura, California, headquarters and its Reno, Nevada, distribution center. While Patagonia parents pay market rates for this service, the company subsidizes a variety of enrichment programs. The Great Pacific Child Development Center (at Patagonia's headquarters) includes a rock-climbing wall, playground, mud kitchen, and garden, and it offers afterschool programs and even a summer surfing camp to its charges, which number about 100 kids ranging from infant to 9 years old. According to former CEO Rose Marcario, JPMorgan Chase determined that Patagonia was getting a 115 percent return on its childcare investment and KPMG calculated that Patagonia's clients received a 125 percent return on their daycare programs.[28] It's perhaps no surprise that a survey of Patagonia conducted by Great Place to Work found that 91 percent of employees report that the company is a "great place to work." Contrast this with just 59 percent for the average American company.[29]

Goldman Sachs set up a $500 million loan fund to provide small businesses in need throughout the United States with emergency aid. The loans were rapidly deployed to underserved communities and issued through the bank's established network of community development financial institutions (CDFIs) across the country. According to Goldman Sachs, more than 8,000 small businesses were reached with an average loan size of $61,285 and 49 percent of the capital was deployed in majority minority areas.[30]

While blending life and work have always been challenging for dual-career couples, the COVID-19 pandemic exposed these families to far more stress, with some parents having to quit their jobs to cover all the bases. According to a survey published by the parenting benefits platform Cleo in July 2020, 27 percent of respondents said they planned to quit their jobs due to the pressures of parenting through the pandemic.[31] The burden has fallen particularly hard on women. According to a *Washington Post* article, "The pandemic has wiped out job gains women made over the past decade, just months after women reached the majority of the paid workforce for only the second time in American history."[32]

Anaplan did just about everything it could think of to put employees' safety and well-being first, which included extending various forms of flexibility and support. Recognizing the particular strain on caregivers, we piloted a flexible-work program that allowed employees to temporarily reduce their hours or opt for a part-time schedule in order to better manage the different demands in their lives.

COVID-19 has also led many people to rethink where they work and live; with remote work becoming the norm and zero desire to resume long commutes, some are opting to relocate to less congested or less expensive areas, or to be closer to family networks. Anaplan is creating guidelines for location flexibility, allowing employees to relocate temporarily or permanently in response to these trends. If work is "not a place you go, but a set of outcomes you achieve," as Marilyn Miller likes to describe it, we can treat the pandemic not as an interruption to the status quo but as an opportunity for innovative new ways of working going forward.

I'm proud to say Anaplan leaned into our company character during the pandemic lockdowns, and we saw benefits I couldn't have imagined. In balancing the risk-reward equation to our business, we learned it wasn't risky to do things that we wouldn't do in normal times. Because of our foundation of character—being values-led and empathetic to the employee experience—we were comfortable taking the risk because we believed the employee experience was paramount. Given the context, our character became more equity-fluent.

I've also been impressed by Adobe's work on reimagining the employee experience for the future of work. Gloria Chen, Adobe's Chief People Officer, has developed a vision based on extensive research with leaders across Adobe, augmented by employee surveys. The company has contextualized the work to the needs of its business, external macrotrends, and standard for an equitable, inclusive culture.

The Adobe Future of Work vision reads: *The future of work is flexible and hybrid, enabled by a digital-first mindset*, prioritizing three key points:

1. Empowering teams to define how and where they work best, while providing individuals with as much flexibility as possible;
2. An intentional mix of physical and virtual presence, with real life gatherings driven by purpose and designed for inclusion; and
3. Virtual workflows as our new norm—from meetings and documentation, to knowledge-sharing and career development.

Like so many businesses reliant on teams of knowledge workers, Adobe's 22,000 employees shifted to primarily working from home in early 2020. While its culture of creativity and innovation drove the resilience to transition productively, and demand for Adobe's digital workflow products soared, Chen says Adobe quickly realized adapting to sustained digital-first work required holistic rethinking of its workplace practices and policies.

Chen is leading an extraordinary and comprehensive redefining of a fundamentally digital employee experience. What stands out for me about Adobe's approach is its roots in equity and inclusion. The company is thinking about how a hybrid presence—working from home with occasional in-person collaborative and culture-building experiences—can help every employee thrive while strengthening agility, creativity, and innovation. It is investing in training, tools, and resources for leaders, managers, and teams to work, develop, and grow their careers in a hybrid workplace. And Adobe is accommodating the reality that flexibility will be a top criterion for all employees.

I firmly believe that we as employers must help our people find the blend they need to take care of their work *and* themselves and their families. We must also ensure that leaders are empathetic and well versed in different life experiences and backgrounds—this will go a long way toward creating a truly inclusive workplace culture where everyone can succeed. The workplace of the future must be equity-fluent.

Becoming an Equity-fluent Leader

According to Professor Kellie McElhaney, becoming an equity-fluent leader requires a lot of self-work; it's not for the faint of heart or for people who want to just take an unconscious bias training class and then tick it off of their list. She offers the following suggestions as a starting point for anyone who is committed to becoming an equity-fluent leader:

- **Be intentionally inclusive.** It has to start with an absolute commitment to the practice. If you don't intentionally include, you unintentionally exclude. Being inclusive isn't something you think; it's something you *do*. It requires *action*.
- **Be curious.** Because of how each of us was raised, we all have blind spots. So, read books that wouldn't be in your normal repertoire, written by people who are different from you. Watch films, read articles, and listen to podcasts by and about people who are different from you. Follow Instagram influencers who are different from you. We all learn in different ways, so whatever way works for you, just go study.
- **Stop talking and listen**. Spend as much time as possible with people who are as different as possible from you in terms of your own set of identities. Ask them about their lived experience and then do nothing but shut up and listen.
- **Examine your biases.** Name a bias that you have. Biases are based on two factors: past experience or cultural stereotypes. Start with something low-stakes and then dissect that bias. For example, you might find that you are biased against men with beards because your former boss with a beard routinely took credit for your work. Next, write down your ugliest, most harmful bias and dissect that. Where did it come from? Write it down on a piece of paper and put it in your pocket or wallet and carry it around for 24 hours, then take note of how the exercise made you feel.[33]

My Greatest Hope

As we think about the future of work, know that what we do *today* determines tomorrow. That's why upstanding character is so urgently relevant now.

The people we depend on for our businesses to win—employees, customers, investors, and communities—expect upstanding character. They *want* us to do what's right. They're *depending* on us to do what's right.

Thinking about the future always makes me think about my kids. My daughter is 17 and finishing high school. Like so many parents with kids transitioning to adult life, I'm having a lot of conversations with her about college, career, and life choices. She and my 14-year-old son are interested in this book and what company character really means. They've both grown up with diverse families and friends in their lives, and naturally embrace racial and gender identity differences, social justice, and equity. I can see my dad's work ethic in them, and I'm looking forward to seeing whom they become being enriched by their expectation for inclusion and integrity. Their optimism and aspirations fuel my conviction that organizations with upstanding character can and must flourish.

With our political landscape continuing to polarize communities in the United States and around the world, companies can lead by uniting people through shared values and objectives that advance a purpose beyond their business mission. It's up to us to create a real sense of belonging for each and every person we hire—and to demonstrate inclusivity with all of our stakeholders, internal and external.

No one has a monopoly on upstanding character, and there's no secret recipe for success. It's simply a matter of embodying your stated values—ensuring what you say and do are aligned, and living out your unique version of an upstanding character, every day.

Professor Kellie McElhaney boiled it down to these three simple statements that summarize what it feels like when you use upstanding character to create a true sense of belonging for everyone in your organization:

> *I feel seen. I can be my full and authentic self here.*
> *I feel heard. My opinions and contributions matter.*
> *I feel valued. I am supported and my team looks out for me.*

No matter what your position may be in an organization—from CEO or board member to frontline employee, and everyone in between—be sure you keep these three statements in mind as you work with everyone you interact with, both inside and outside your organization.

Our Chief Customer Officer recently told me about the outcome of a five-hour customer presentation. After the presentation, the executive sponsor said, "You are not in the technology business, you are in the *hope business* because you make my hope real."[34] Ultimately, it's hope that drives us forward—hope to become better people, hope to provide increased value to our customers, hope to leave the world a better place than we found it.

Now that we have reached the end of this book, I have a few questions for you:

What will you do, starting right now, to activate your character—to take it from offline to online?

What will you do to be more accountable to yourself—and to others?

What will you do to influence the people you work with to join with you to activate their own character?

We are at an inflection point like no other. If your company takes character for granted, you will be defeated by your competition; you will become irrelevant to your employees or your customers. The stakes for company character have never been higher.

People are demanding their leader's social conscience—a moral mirror—be actively displayed, blurring conventional distinctions between personal and professional convictions. The old way of compartmentalizing our personal opinions on social issues is long gone. The impersonal, indifferent leader is an outdated ethos. The contemporary, and I would argue competitive, way of leading in business must start with an activated, online upstanding character—authentic, inclusive, and empathetic. This mindset will now begin to distinguish your ability to succeed just as much as your professional skillset, education, and experience.

Character-led culture has never been more vital than it is today. I strongly urge you to take advantage of this moment. If you don't show up with empathy and agility, the person or company who does will eclipse you. But, if you build the qualities that demonstrate *upstanding company character*, your organization will win today and sustain its advantages well into the future.

Upstanding companies endure.

Upstanding Character Defined

Upstanding character is the set of traits essential for leaders and organizations that want advantage-gaining connection and relevance with stakeholders. These traits guide behavior while embracing what has always been good for business: the pursuit of excellence, respect for individuals, and community engagement. Upstanding character is values-led and advances shared purpose.

Leaders with upstanding company character are authentic and accountable, have clear personal convictions and a growth mindset, and foster inclusivity. Organizations with upstanding character:

- **Operate with larger purpose.** Their company purpose is clear and shared. They aim to create value for all stakeholders, including employees, customers, partners, investors, and the communities in which they operate. They stand for a set of environmental, social, and governance convictions aligned with their purpose and values.
- **Are values-led.** These organizations define, communicate, and reinforce strong core values that are universally recognized, used for decision-making, and guide collective behavior.
- **Follow through on convictions.** They consistently—perhaps *obsessively*—insist on doing what they say they are going to do. They are mindful that stakeholder trust is tied to their accountability to their purpose, convictions, and commitments, and their alignment to their convictions on environmental, social, and governance issues.
- **Answer the call in challenging times.** When confronted with a crisis, these companies will answer the call—making hard decisions and navigating uncertainty guided by the upstanding traits embedded in their DNA.

Endnotes

Introduction

1. https://archive.fortune.com/magazines/fortune/fortune500_archive/full/1979/
2. https://www.ibm.com/ibm/history/history/year_1962.html
3. https://www.cambridge.org/core/journals/business-history-review/article/change-and-continuity-at-ibm-key-themes-in-histories-of-ibm/DADE64D DC8569B2F9046B4CF47DFA814/core-reader
4. https://www.economist.com/news/2008/07/28/downsizing
5. https://www.cnet.com/news/ciscos-chambers-cuts-salary-to-1/
6. https://www.bloomberg.com/news/articles/2003-11-23/ciscos-comeback

Chapter 1

1. https://www.zerohedge.com/markets/mortgage-delinquencies-plus-90-days-due-hits-decade-high
2. https://www.cnbc.com/2020/08/25/american-airlines-is-cutting-19000-jobs-when-federal-aid-expires-in-october.html
3. https://sanfrancisco.cbslocal.com/2020/08/24/more-than-half-of-san-francisco-storefronts-closed-due-to-pandemic/
4. https://www.wto.org/english/news_e/pres20_e/pr855_e.htm
5. https://blog.perceptyx.com/just-4-percent-of-employees-want-to-return-to-the-office-full-time
6. https://www.gallup.com/workplace/232958/bring-best-people-company.aspx
7. https://smith.queensu.ca/magazine/issues/winter-2014/features/engaging-employees.php
8. https://www.strategyand.pwc.com/global-culture-survey
9. https://www.gallup.com/workplace/236351/star-employees-slipping-away.aspx
10. https://www.glassdoor.com/research/employee-satisfaction-drivers/
11. https://www.glassdoor.com/about-us/workplace-culture-over-salary/

12. Richard Sterba, "Character and Resistance," *The Psychoanalytic Quarterly*, 20:1 (1951) 72–76, DOI:10.1080/21674086.1951.11925832

13. https://www.greatplacetowork.com/best-workplaces/100-best/2020

14. Ibid.

15. https://www.economist.com/briefing/2016/09/03/from-zero-to-seventy-billion

16. https://moveme.berkeley.edu/project/deleteuber/

17. https://www.bloomberg.com/news/features/2018-01-18/the-fall-of-travis-kalanick-was-a-lot-weirder-and-darker-than-you-thought

18. Sara Baxter Orr interview with Frank Calderoni: September 18, 2020.

19. Ray Curbelo interview with Frank Calderoni: September 18, 2020.

20. Claire Lord interview with Frank Calderoni: September 18, 2020.

21. AKO/FY20, Anaplan Kickoff Day 1

22. https://sloanreview.mit.edu/culture500/research

Chapter 2

1. https://strategiesforinfluence.com/crossing-the-chasm-geoffrey-moore/

2. https://www.communication-director.com/issues/working-relationship/jon-iwata/#.XvPMnZNKiNg

3. https://www.pewresearch.org/fact-tank/2020/06/09/hispanic-women-immigrants-young-adults-those-with-less-education-hit-hardest-by-covid-19-job-losses/

4. https://fortune.com/2020/03/16/coronavirus-stock-market-news-dow-jones-sp-500-drop/

5. We have used a pseudonym to protect his privacy.

6. Omar Abbosh interview with Frank Calderoni: September 14, 2020.

7. https://www.owllabs.com/state-of-remote-work#:~:text=Remote%20Work%20Statistics-,1.,at%20a%20fully%2Dremote%20company.

8. https://www.gallup.com/workplace/283985/working-remotely-effective-gallup-research-says-yes.aspx

9. https://news.gallup.com/poll/306695/workers-discovering-affinity-remote-work.aspx

10. https://www.cnn.com/2020/05/22/tech/work-from-home-companies/index.html

11. https://twitter.com/tobi/status/1263483496087064579

12. https://radio.wosu.org/post/nationwide-moves-smaller-regional-offices-permanent-remote-work#stream/0

13. https://content.ebulletins.com/hubfs/C1/Culture%20Wizard/LL-2018%20Trends%20in%20Global%20VTs%20Draft%2012%20and%20a%20half.pdf

14. https://www.bls.gov/news.release/tenure.nr0.htm

15. https://www.payscale.com/data-packages/employee-loyalty/full-list

16. https://www.zdnet.com/article/us-companies-facing-a-huge-tech-talent-deficit-in-2020/

17. https://scholarship.law.georgetown.edu/legal/50/

18. https://www.bls.gov/ncs/ebs/benefits/2019/ownership/private/table02a.pdf

19. https://www.greatplacetowork.com/resources/blog/6-elements-of-great-company-culture

20. Cy Wakeman, *The Reality-Based Rules of the Workplace*, Jossey-Bass (2013), p. 2.

21. http://www.realitybasedleadership.com/wp-content/uploads/2017/03/Reality-Based-Philosophy-Certification-Program-Description.pdf

22. https://www.cnet.com/news/oracles-ellison-nails-cloud-computing/

23. https://www.statista.com/statistics/233725/development-of-amazon-web-services-revenue/

24. https://www.zdnet.com/article/aws-brings-in-nearly-10b-in-sales-for-amazon-in-q4/

25. https://www.statista.com/statistics/477277/cloud-infrastructure-services-market-share/

26. https://www.latimes.com/business/story/2019-11-05/column-data-brokers

27. https://learning.blogs.nytimes.com/2012/01/05/jan-5-1914-henry-ford-implements-5-a-day-wage/

28. https://www.uschamberfoundation.org/blog/post/how-business-s-good-character-gets-job-done/31607

Chapter 3

1. Yvonne Wassenaar interview with Frank Calderoni: June 15, 2020.

2. https://s22.q4cdn.com/422360030/files/doc_downloads/governance/2019-Anaplan-Code-of-Conduct-and-Ethics-(Final)[2].pdf

3. https://www.mckinsey.com/featured-insights/diversity-and-inclusion/diversity-wins-how-inclusion-matters

4. https://www.conference-board.org/pdf_free/councils/TCBCP009.pdf

5. https://www.adobe.com/aboutadobe/pressroom/pdfs/Adobe_State_of_Create_Infographic.pdf

6. https://www.corporatecomplianceinsights.com/right-thing-ethics-corruption-compliance/

7. Cy Wakeman interview with Frank Calderoni: July 15, 2020.

8. https://www.nytimes.com/2020/08/14/opinion/pinterest-discrimination-women.html

9. Ibid.

10. Cy Wakeman interview with Frank Calderoni: August 17, 2020.

11. Ibid.

12. https://medium.com/@CyWakeman/redefining-accountability-in-the-workplace-1e880b4246d6

13. Marilyn Miller interview with Frank Calderoni: June 15, 2020.
14. https://www.mckinsey.com/featured-insights/diversity-and-inclusion/diversity-wins-how-inclusion-matters
15. https://hbr.org/2016/01/what-having-a-growth-mindset-actually-means

Chapter 4

1. https://www.coca-colacompany.com/brands
2. https://learn.interbrand.com/hubfs/INTERBRAND/Interbrand_Best_Global_Brands%202020%20Desktop.pdf
3. https://us.coca-cola.com/together/
4. Ibid.
5. https://www.coca-colacompany.com/news/where-we-stand-on-social-justice
6. Victor Barnes interview with Frank Calderoni: June 17, 2020.
7. https://www.nytimes.com/1964/12/29/archives/tribute-to-dr-king-disputed-in-atlanta.html
8. https://www.ajc.com/news/king-nobel-challenged-atlanta-tolerance/bExE4m07T4KCuOD88E3diK/
9. https://knowledge.page.org/report/corporate-character-how-leading-companies-are-defining-activating-aligning-values/
10. https://www.mayoclinic.org/healthy-lifestyle/consumer-health/in-depth/mindfulness-exercises/art-20046356
11. Doug Merritt interview with Frank Calderoni: July 20, 2020.
12. Ibid.
13. Sara Park interview with Frank Calderoni: June 24, 2020.

Chapter 5

1. https://hbr.org/2009/05/what-only-the-ceo-can-do
2. https://fortune.com/2009/06/09/pgs-lafley-lessons-in-leadership/
3. https://hbr.org/2009/05/what-only-the-ceo-can-do
4. James Collins and Jerry Porras, "Building Your Company's Vision," *Harvard Business Review* (September–October 1996).
5. https://www.kornferry.com/insights/articles/575-the-purpose-of-strategy-is-to-win-an-interview-with-a-g-lafley
6. https://www.washingtonpost.com/national/robert-mcdonald-obamas-va-nominee-faced-own-challenges-at-procter-and-gamble/2014/07/01/0211a90a-009e-11e4-8572-4b1b969b6322_story.html
7. https://www.forbes.com/sites/jeremybogaisky/2013/05/23/bob-mcdonald-out-at-procter-a-g-lafley-returning-as-ceo/#7e04a4737309

8. https://www.cincinnati.com/story/money/2016/06/01/lafley-leaving-pg-end-june/85258750/

9. Laura Desmond interview with Frank Calderoni: June 30, 2020.

10. James Collins and Jerry Porras, "Building Your Company's Vision," *Harvard Business Review* (September–October 1996).

11. https://qz.com/1740791/can-uber-overcome-years-of-toxicity-coursing-through-its-company/

12. Brad Stone, *The Upstarts: How Uber, Airbnb, and the Killer Companies of the New Silicon Valley Are Changing the World*, Little, Brown and Company (2017), p. 316.

13. Ibid., p. 317.

14. https://www.uber.com/newsroom/company-info/

15. https://www.linkedin.com/pulse/ubers-new-cultural-norms-dara-khosrowshahi/

16. https://www.cnet.com/news/ubers-u-turn-how-ceo-dara-khosrowshahi-is-cleaning-up-after-scandals-and-lawsuits/

17. https://www.linkedin.com/pulse/ubers-new-cultural-norms-dara-khosrowshahi/

18. https://www.wired.com/story/uber-move-slow-test-things/

19. 2019 Employee Engagement Trends, Quantum Workplace (2019) https://marketing.quantumworkplace.com/hubfs/Marketing/Website/Resources/PDFs/2019-Employee-Engagement-Trends-Report.pdf

20. Interview Geoffrey Moore with Frank Calderoni: July 20, 2020.

21. https://money.cnn.com/2015/07/31/technology/uber-50-billion-valuation/index.html#:~:text=Uber%20is%20now%20the%20most,at%20close%20to%20%2451%20billion

22. https://money.cnn.com/2018/08/29/technology/uber-ceo-dara-khosrowshahi-one-year-anniversary/index.html

23. https://hbr.org/2016/03/two-thirds-of-managers-are-uncomfortable-communicating-with-employees

24. https://rework.withgoogle.com/guides/managers-identify-what-makes-a-great-manager/steps/learn-about-googles-manager-research/

25. Interview Tiger Tyagarajan with Frank Calderoni: July 14, 2020.

26. Ibid.

27. https://www.investors.com/news/management/leaders-and-success/adobe-ceo-shows-you-surpass-status-quo/

28. Interview Shantanu Narayen with Frank Calderoni: July 16, 2020.

Chapter 6

1. https://www.marketwatch.com/story/netflix-shares-close-up-8-for-yet-another-record-high-2020-07-10

2. Reed Hastings and Erin Meyer, *No Rules Rules: Netflix and the Culture of Reinvention*, Penguin Press (2020), p. xiii.

3. https://jobs.netflix.com/culture

4. Reed Hastings and Erin Meyer, *No Rules Rules: Netflix and the Culture of Reinvention*, Penguin Press (2020), p. xix.

5. Ibid., p. xix–xx

6. https://www.slideshare.net/reed2001/culture-1798664/2-Netflix_Culture-Freedom_Responsibility2

7. https://techcrunch.com/2013/01/31/read-what-facebooks-sandberg-calls-maybe-the-most-important-document-ever-to-come-out-of-the-valley/

8. https://firstround.com/review/The-woman-behind-the-Netflix-Culture-doc/

9. https://knowledge.wharton.upenn.edu/article/how-netflix-built-its-company-culture/

10. Ibid.

11. Reed Hastings and Erin Meyer, *No Rules Rules: Netflix and the Culture of Reinvention*, Penguin Press (2020), p. xxi.

12. Patty McCord, *Powerful: Building a Culture of Freedom and Responsibility*, Missionday, LLC, Kindle Edition, p. 14.

13. https://hired.com/page/brand-health-report/top-global-employer-brands

14. https://www.marketwatch.com/investing/stock/nflx/financials

15. https://www.nytimes.com/2020/04/21/business/media/netflix-q1-2020-earnings-nflx.html

16. https://www.ft.com/content/822ed110-0f3d-11de-ba10-0000779fd2ac

17. https://www.businessroundtable.org/about-us

18. https://www.businessroundtable.org/business-roundtable-redefines-the-purpose-of-a-corporation-to-promote-an-economy-that-serves-all-americans

19. https://www2.deloitte.com/content/dam/Deloitte/us/Documents/about-deloitte/us-leadership-2014-core-beliefs-culture-survey-040414.pdf

20. https://www2.deloitte.com/global/en/pages/about-deloitte/articles/millennialsurvey.html

21. Kirsten Rhodes interview with Frank Calderoni: September 24, 2020.

22. https://www.cisco.com/en/US/services/ps2961/ps2664/collaborative_imperative.pdf

23. Simon Tucker interview with Frank Calderoni: September 11, 2020.

24. Melissa Schwartz interview with Frank Calderoni: September 24, 2020.

25. Deb Kennedy interview with Frank Calderoni: September 24, 2020.

26. Allison Grieb interview with Frank Calderoni: September 24, 2020.

27. Ana Pinczuk interview with Frank Calderoni: September 11, 2020.

28. Doug Merritt interview with Frank Calderoni: July 20, 2020.

29. Ibid.

30. https://www.annualreports.com/HostedData/AnnualReports/PDF/NYSE_DIS_2019.pdf

31. https://disneyparks.disney.go.com/blog/2011/01/how-do-we-give-every-disney-dream-guest-an-ocean-view-its-magic/

32. Marilyn Miller interview with Frank Calderoni: June 15, 2020.

33. Marilyn Miller interview with Frank Calderoni: June 15, 2020.
34. https://www.apple.com/jobs/us/

Chapter 7

1. https://www.cpapracticeadvisor.com/accounting-audit/news/21160049/expensify-ceo-sends-email-to-10-million-customers-urging-a-vote-for-biden
2. https://blog.coinbase.com/coinbase-is-a-mission-focused-company-af882df8804
3. https://www.theatlantic.com/ideas/archive/2020/10/should-professional-be-political/616810/
4. https://www.linkedin.com/in/frankacalderoni/detail/recent-activity/shares/
5. https://www.leverage2lead.com
6. https://theconversation.com/corporate-activism-is-more-than-a-marketing-gimmick-141570
7. https://www.nytimes.com/2020/08/14/opinion/pinterest-discrimination-women.html
8. https://medium.com/digital-diplomacy/the-pinterest-paradox-cupcakes-and-toxicity-57ed6bd76960
9. Ibid.
10. Complaint for Damages, Demand for Jury Trial: Francoise Brougher vs. Pinterest Inc., Case No. CGC-20-585888, Superior Court of the State of California, In and for the County of San Francisco, p. 12. Retrieved from https://docplayer.net/191786225-Francoise-brougher-complains-and-alleges-as-follows-nature-of-the-case.html
11. https://www.nytimes.com/2020/08/14/opinion/pinterest-discrimination-women.html
12. https://www.businessinsider.com/pinterest-francoise-brougher-gender-discrimination-suit-coo-2020-12
13. https://www.paradigm4parity.com/#intro
14. https://www.paradigm4parity.com/solution#plan
15. Matthew Jordan interview with Frank Calderoni: September 16, 2020.
16. Sara Park interview with Frank Calderoni: June 24, 2020.
17. https://www.pwc.co.uk/human-resource-services/assets/documents/real-diversity-2017-no-holding-back.pdf
18. Yvonne Wassenaar interview with Frank Calderoni: June 15, 2020.
19. YY Lee interview with Frank Calderoni: May 28, 2020.
20. https://firstround.com/review/40-favorite-interview-questions-from-some-of-the-sharpest-folks-we-know/
21. Ibid.
22. Ibid.

23. https://www.nytimes.com/2013/06/20/business/in-head-hunting-big-data-may-not-be-such-a-big-deal.html
24. https://careersidekick.com/brain-teaser-job-interview-questions-facebook-google-apple/
25. https://www.nytimes.com/2013/06/20/business/in-head-hunting-big-data-may-not-be-such-a-big-deal.html
26. https://firstround.com/review/40-favorite-interview-questions-from-some-of-the-sharpest-folks-we-know/
27. Sue Bostrom interview with Frank Calderoni: July 16, 2020.
28. Ibid.
29. Ibid.
30. Tilt365, True Tilt Personality Profile, Tilt365 Positive Influence Predictor are trademarks of Tilt, Inc. Used with permission.
31. https://www.tilt365.com/Portals/0/LiveKnowledgebase/802/true-tilt-profile-spec-sheet-3-12-18-blk-txt-b1.pdf

Chapter 8

1. https://www.instagram.com/p/CBEcwTgneUY/
2. https://www.instagram.com/p/CBJrhdzHKNt/
3. https://hbr.org/2020/11/what-an-anti-racist-business-strategy-looks-like
4. https://www.blog.google/inside-google/company-announcements/standing-with-black-community/
5. https://alexisohanian.com/home/2020/6/5/what-did-you-do
6. Marc Benioff and Monica Langley, *Trailblazer: The Power of Business as the Greatest Platform for Change*, Currency (2019), p. 7.
7. https://cvshealth.com/news-and-insights/press-releases/cvs-health-to-provide-bonuses-add-benefits-and-hire-50000-in
8. Ibid.
9. https://edition.cnn.com/2020/03/15/business/coronavirus-lvmh-dior-hand-sanitizer-trnd/index.html
10. https://www.weforum.org/agenda/2020/07/companies-action-support-covid-19-response/
11. Marilyn Miller interview with Frank Calderoni: June 15, 2020.
12. https://www.linkedin.com/pulse/i-pledge-support-my-fellow-ibmers-working-from-home-during-krishna/
13. Ibid.
14. https://sustainablebrands.com/read/marketing-and-comms/new-report-reveals-86-of-us-consumers-expect-companies-to-act-on-social-environmental-issues
15. Ibid.
16. Sue Bostrom interview with Frank Calderoni: July 16, 2020.

17. https://ballotpedia.org/California_Proposition_8,_the_%22Eliminates_Right_of_Same-Sex_Couples_to_Marry%22_Initiative_(2008)
18. Sue Bostrom interview with Frank Calderoni: July 16, 2020.
19. https://www.investopedia.com/articles/personal-finance/071415/how-nba-makes-money.asp
20. https://www.charlottemagazine.com/hb2-how-north-carolina-got-here-updated/
21. https://www.washingtonpost.com/news/sports/wp/2016/07/21/report-nba-will-move-2017-all-star-game-from-charlotte-to-new-orleans-over-hb2-law/
22. https://www.npr.org/sections/thetwo-way/2017/03/27/521676772/ap-calculates-north-carolinas-bathroom-bill-will-cost-more-than-3-7-billion
23. Eric Hutcherson interview with Frank Calderoni: August 5, 2020.
24. http://global.nba.com/news/nba-statement-regarding-2017-nba-all-star-game/
25. Eric Hutcherson interview with Frank Calderoni: August 5, 2020.
26. Ibid.
27. Sara Baxter Orr and Eric Hutcherson (September 10, 2020). CFO + CHRO Mandate: A Conversation with the NBA's Head of HR. Retrieved from: https://youtu.be/ziGfbvANmCQ

Chapter 9

1. Shantanu Narayen interview with Frank Calderoni: July 16, 2020.
2. Yvonne Wassenaar interview with Frank Calderoni: June 15, 2020.
3. Sara Park interview with Frank Calderoni: June 24, 2020.
4. Victor Barnes interview with Frank Calderoni: June 17, 2020.
5. https://jobs.chegg.com/why-work-at-chegg
6. Dan Rosensweig interview with Frank Calderoni: June 23, 2020.
7. Allan Leinwand interview with Frank Calderoni: June 17, 2020.
8. Elizabeth King interview with Frank Calderoni: June 26, 2020.
9. Tiger Tyagarajan interview with Frank Calderoni: July 14, 2020.
10. https://www.forbes.com/sites/danschawbel/2013/05/28/cy-wakeman-how-to-evaluate-the-roi-of-an-employee/#6b6e70967c3e
11. Tiger Tyagarajan interview with Frank Calderoni: July 14, 2020.
12. Doug Merritt interview with Frank Calderoni: July 20, 2020.
13. Mike Tickle interview with Frank Calderoni: August 18, 2020.

Chapter 10

1. https://www.mckinsey.com/featured-insights/diversity-and-inclusion/diversity-still-matters
2. https://cacm.acm.org/careers/240175-americas-got-talent-just-not-enough-in-it/fulltext

3. https://www.globenewswire.com/fr/news-release/2020/08/18/2079987/0/en/
   Fortinet-and-IBM-Collaborate-on-SkillsBuild-to-Further-Build-Cybersecurity-
   Skills.html
4. https://www.cnbc.com/2018/05/30/silicon-valley-is-stumped-even-a-i-cannot-
   remove-bias-from-hiring.html
5. https://hbswk.hbs.edu/item/minorities-who-whiten-job-resumes-get-more-
   interviews
6. https://trywebassess.com/myinnergenius-assessments/
7. https://www.cnbc.com/2019/10/03/why-ibm-is-using-ai-to-find-jobs-for-people-
   without-college-degree.html
8. Ibid.
9. https://www.nytimes.com/2019/09/17/style/generation-z-millennials-work-life-
   balance.html
10. https://blog.linkedin.com/2018/june/26/workplace-culture-trends-the-key-to-
    hiring-and-keeping-top-talent
11. https://www.cnbc.com/2018/06/27/nearly-9-out-of-10-millennials-would-consider-
    a-pay-cut-to-get-this.html
12. https://blog.linkedin.com/2018/june/26/workplace-culture-trends-the-key-to-
    hiring-and-keeping-top-talent
13. https://www.gallup.com/workplace/316064/employee-engagement-hits-new-
    high-historic-drop.aspx
14. https://www.gallup.com/workplace/284180/factors-driving-record-high-
    employee-engagement.aspx
15. Ibid.
16. https://barryoreilly.com/the-certainties-of-uncertainty/
17. Ibid.
18. Marilyn Miller interview with Frank Calderoni: June 15, 2020.
19. https://www.prnewswire.com/news-releases/top-business-leaders-launch-
    oneten-301190346.html
20. Ibid.
21. https://www.wsj.com/articles/ceos-pledge-one-million-jobs-for-black-
    americans-11607601610
22. Kellie McElhaney interview with Frank Calderoni: August 22, 2020.
23. https://haas.berkeley.edu/equity/industry/playbooks/
24. Genevieve Smith and Ishita Rustagi, "Supporting Dual Career Couples: An Equity
    Fluent Leadership Playbook Executive Summary," Center for Equity, Gender &
    Leadership (2020), p. 3.
25. Ibid., p. 1.
26. Ibid., p. 4.
27. Abigail Mackey, Kellie McElhaney, and Genevieve Smith, "Transforming Business
    Beyond COVID-19: An Equity Fluent Leadership Playbook," Center for Equity,
    Gender & Leadership (2020), p. 28.

28. https://business.linkedin.com/talent-solutions/blog/company-culture/2019/ why-patagonia-offers-onsite-child-care
29. https://www.greatplacetowork.com/certified-company/1000745
30. https://www.goldmansachs.com/citizenship/10000-small-businesses/US/ infographic-commitment-across-us/index.html
31. https://fortune.com/2020/07/14/childcare-working-parents-coronavirus-survey-cleo/
32. https://www.washingtonpost.com/dc-md-va/2020/05/09/women-unemployment-jobless-coronavirus/
33. Kellie McElhaney interview with Frank Calderoni: August 22, 2020.
34. Email from Christophe Bodin: September 11, 2020.

Acknowledgments

So many people have helped me, not only with this book but with my journey as a business leader throughout my career. I have been fortunate to have had so many special experiences and professional relationships over the years. I am grateful to the several great companies I worked for that afforded me those opportunities.

I want to first thank everyone who so generously agreed to allow me to interview them and include some of their insights on character in the book: Sue Bostrom, Allan Leinwand, and Yvonne Wassenaar are members of the Anaplan board of directors whose advice and judgment I am always grateful for; Tiger Tyagarajan, Doug Merritt, Dan Rosensweig, and Shantanu Narayen are all CEO peers whom I greatly admire (with additional thanks to Shantanu—a trusted colleague, friend, and down-to-earth kind of guy who brings his personal traits of humility and respect to the Adobe culture, and who also penned the Foreword for this book); Elizabeth King, Laura Desmond, Omar Abbosh, and Eric Hutcherson are all business leaders I have been fortunate to know; and Victor Barnes, Sara Park, and Mike Tickle are all valued Anaplan customers. I also want to thank Geoffrey Moore for his business insights; Cy Wakeman for her expertise and coaching on Reality-Based Leadership; Kellie McElhaney for her thoughts on equity-fluent leadership and partnership on the belonging index; Pam Boney, originator of Tilt365; and Kirsten Rhodes, one of our most trusted partners.

Thanks also to the team at Wiley, in particular, Zach Schisgal and Kezia Endsley; and to my literary agent Giles Anderson for your patience and comments and suggestions throughout my journey as a writer.

I also have deep appreciation for my leadership team at Anaplan, in particular, Ana Pinczuk, YY Lee, and Simon Tucker, who shared their thoughts for this book; other key Anaplanners include Sara Baxter Orr, Ray Curbelo, Claire Lord, Deb Kennedy, Melissa Schwartz, and Allison Grieb; Ollie Jones-Taylor and Matthew Jordan, who shared deeply personal stories; Anthony

Harrison for being a critical reader; the creative, dedicated, and supportive core team that provided guidance and structure as I embarked on this project, in particular, Alice Hansen, Grace Prasad, Peter Economy, and Jeanne Rotenberry; and finally, Georgina Brown who designed a beautiful cover, and my photographer Jon Barber.

I want to mention Marilyn Miller separately. She has been simply outstanding as my Chief People Officer during most of my time at Anaplan, but in particular, throughout 2020; and Linda Lee, who has worked with me for many years at three different companies and who offers the tough but necessary feedback that I need to hear.

I would also like to thank AlexSandra Leslie, who has been a wonderful coach to me over the years, and CeCe Rosario, who spent over 10 years working closely with me through many challenging situations and is one of the kindest people I have ever met. I also want to acknowledge all the people whom I have worked for—especially John Chambers. In addition, I owe a debt of gratitude to Georgia Williams, my first mentor at IBM.

To the employees at Anaplan, I cannot say enough how grateful I am to be your leader. You have all taught me how to be more courageous and authentic. I will forever be A-shaped because of each and every one of you. Thanks also to Michael Gould, founder of Anaplan, who has developed one of the most impressive software products in the market today.

And finally, thanks to my family. To my father, who taught me the value of hard work and of always setting the bar high. To my mother, who is the personification of resilience—to this day, I still want to make you proud. To my brothers, Bob and Rick, who both always kept me on my toes, giving me great advice over the years, and fully support me in everything I do. To my wife Brenda, who has been with me through all these lessons—I thank you for being patient and incredibly supportive as I embarked on this journey of learning. You continue to be my best sounding board. And, to Jessica and Matthew, for being my moral compass, my greatest achievement, and my biggest hope for the future. Jess, just keep your curiosity and strive for excellence. Matt, never lose your limitless optimism, happy disposition, and boundless energy.

About the Author

Frank A. Calderoni is the Chief Executive Officer of Anaplan and the chairman of the company's board of directors. Anaplan, Inc. (NYSE: PLAN) is a cloud-native enterprise SaaS company helping global enterprises orchestrate business performance. Leaders across industries rely on its platform—powered by its proprietary Hyperblock® technology—to connect teams, systems, and insights from across their organizations to continuously adapt to change, transform how they operate, and reinvent value creation. San Francisco–based Anaplan has experienced hypergrowth over the past 10 years, and as a startup, the company attained unicorn status in January 2016 when it achieved a valuation of $1.1 billion. Anaplan's current market cap is approximately $10 billion.

Frank is a technology industry veteran with over 35 years of successful executive leadership. Before joining Anaplan, Frank served as the Executive Vice President (EVP), Operations and Chief Financial Officer (CFO) of Red Hat, Inc. from June 2015 to January 2017. He also served as EVP and CFO at Cisco Systems, Inc. for seven years. Prior to that, he served as Cisco's Senior Vice President (SVP), Customer Solutions Finance from June 2007 to February 2008, and Vice President, Worldwide Sales Finance from May 2004 to June 2007. Frank joined Cisco in 2004 from QLogic Corporation, where he was the SVP and CFO. Prior to that, he was the SVP, Finance & Administration, and CFO for SanDisk Corporation. Earlier in his career, he spent 21 years at IBM. Frank previously served on the board of Palo Alto Networks and currently serves on the board of Adobe Systems, Inc.

Frank been recognized by the *San Francisco Business Times* and Larkin Street Youth Services as the 2013 Bay Area CFO of the Year for a Public Company with revenues above $500 million and was considered one of the Best Chief Financial Officers three years in a row in 2012, 2013, and 2014 by *Institutional Investor* magazine. He holds a BS in Finance and Accounting from Fordham University, and an MBA in Finance from Pace University.

Frank is a lifelong devoted runner who also loves to surf and likes his chai extra hot. In his spare time, he enjoys tending his garden and chasing away rabbits.

Index